Moroccan Myths and Legends

Philippe Fix

Moroccan Myths and Legends

*Traditional Stories
collected by
Philippe Fix*

Ragged Bears

First published in 2003 in the United Kingdom by Ragged Bears Ltd,
Nightingale House, Queen Camel, Somerset BA22 7NN

Translated from the French by Janet Shirley
Page setting UK edition: Karen Bale
Photography: Color'Way

French original edition © ÉDITIONS HOËBEKE, PARIS, (2003)
Original title: 'Contes Populaires du Maroc'
Texts: tales selected and adapted by Philippe Fix from popular tales.
Illustrations: Philippe Fix

Printed and bound in France

A CIP record of this book is available from the British Library

ISBN: 1-85714-280-2

Contents

Entertaining tales
The Story of Old Âref ou Aqel *9*
Weeping and Wailing *10*
The Story of Bartal and Jerâda *12*
The Language of the Birds *17*
The Woman and the Cadi *21*
The Stolen Treasure *22*
Wit is the Best Weapon *26*
The Man with a Stupid Wife *29*
Fair Shares *30*
A House Bought in Paradise *31*
Princess Saktsa or Maskoutsa *32*

Shrewd tales
The Barber in Love *39*
Carefree Heart *42*
The Simpleton's Bargains *45*
The Queen and the King who was Amelknani's Son *47*
He Wanted to Marry a Girl who was Well Brought Up *51*

Fantastic tales
The Story of Moulay Mohammed el-Hanach *57*
The Story of the Two Brothers *63*
The House Where You Die *69*
The Girl and the Ogress *72*

Entertaining Tales

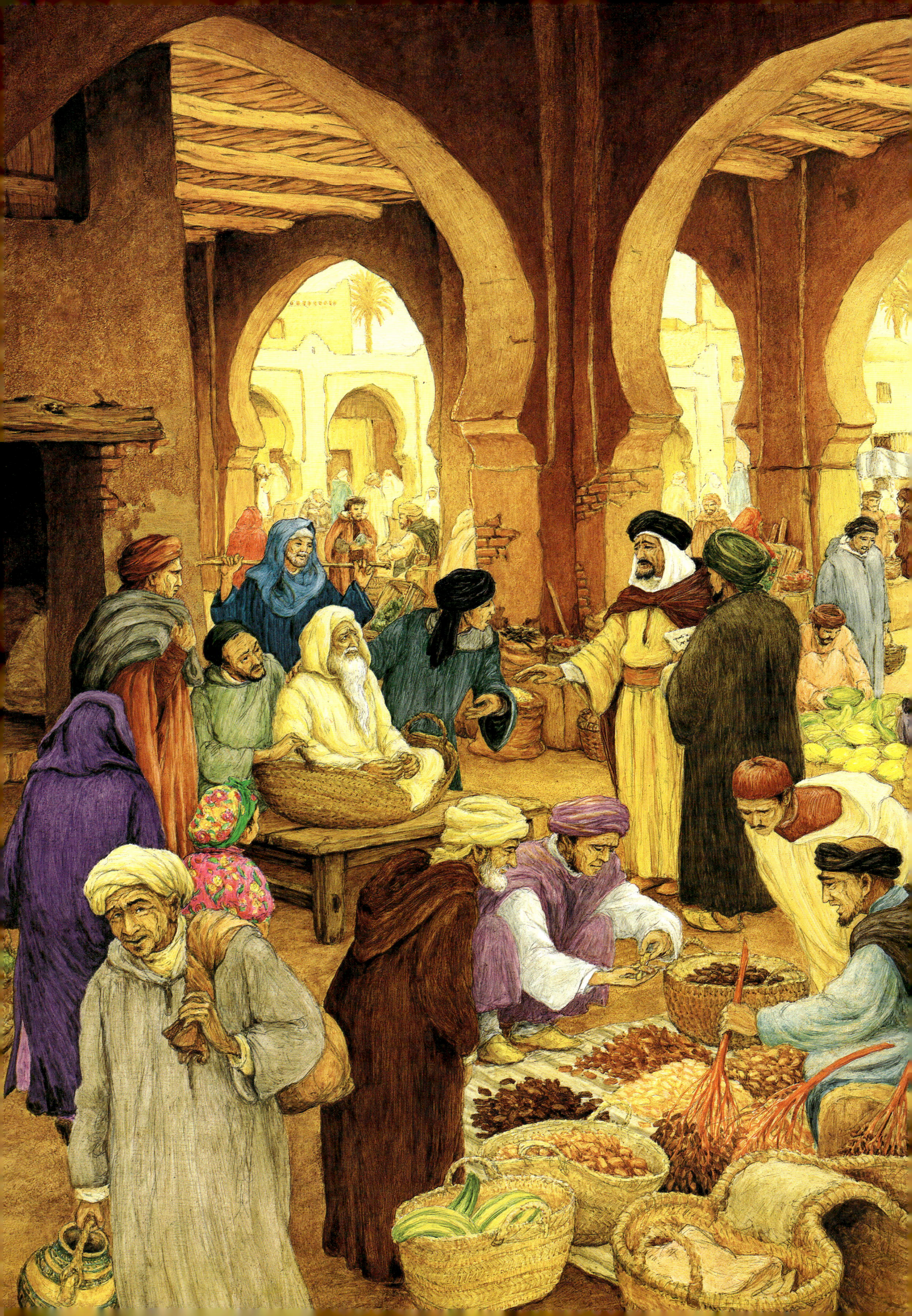

The Story of Old Âref ou Aqel

There was once a man who was over a hundred years old and knew pretty well everything about everything. People called him *'Âref ou Aqel'*, 'the one who knows and understands'.

One day this old man told his sons, 'You must take me to market and sell me at auction, you will do really well out of it.'

At first they would do no such thing, but the old man kept on and kept on at them and at last they agreed. They put him in a big basket and went to market.

And who bought him? It was the king. He gave him a little room in his palace and from that day on he never did anything without asking the old man first. Everything the old man foretold came exactly true, things no one else had known.

One day someone gave the king a pot of honey. He took it to the old man and said,

'What do you think of this? Isn't it the best possible honey?'

'Yes,' answered the old man, 'the flavour is delicious and it's a wonderful colour. But the bees who made it got their pollen in a graveyard.'

And so they had. The king gave the old man a loaf of bread and a bit of roast meat by way of a thank you.

Another time the king was given a wonderful mare, and he showed it to the old man, saying,

'Isn't this a glorious animal?'

'Indeed it is, but it's the only foal its dam ever had, and she was getting old then.'

The king sent for the mare's owner, and he had to admit that what the old man said was true. The king at once had the old man given a loaf of bread and a bit of roast meat for a thank you.

Last of all the king married a young girl, famous for her beauty and goodness, and he wanted to know what the old man thought of his bride. He took her to him. The man who knew and understood looked carefully at her and said,

'Indeed she is lovely, you could not have chosen better. But her mother was not all she should have been when she was young.'

The king was furiously angry and he threatened the old man,

'If you're lying, my executioner shall kill you.' But the old man had told the truth, and the king sent him another loaf and a bit of roast meat.

The sons went to see their father and complained:

'We're going to take you home, this king is too mean to give you anything but bread and roast meat.'

Then their father said to them,

'A man only gives what he can. But what can the son of a baker girl and a roast lamb salesman give except bread and roast meat?'

The king overheard this and he rushed to his mother.

'Tell me at once whose son I am!' he commanded. Trembling, the poor woman admitted, 'You are not my son. We weren't able to have children. But the king, my husband, was going to send me away if I did not give him an heir, so I pretended I was pregnant, I pretended to have the baby, and I gave you to him. You had just been born to my baker girl and your real father, the roast lamb salesman.'

Then the king gave the old man a huge sum of money and magnificent presents and ordered him and his sons to go right away out of that country so that no one should ever know.

Weeping and Wailing

There was once a very poor man who had a great many children to maintain. He was out one day looking for work to feed his family, when he met an old man who said,

'Would you like to come and work for us?'

'What sort of work?'

'You would just go and buy food for us every day, and you would be paid as much as you like.'

He followed the old man, who took him to a house where there was a collection of old men who did nothing but weep and wail. They seemed to be very rich, as all the rooms were full of gold and silver and jewels.

'You can take anything you like from any of these rooms,' said the old man, 'except from that one, and I advise you never to open that door.'

And he rejoined the other old men and they all wept and wailed together.

From then on, the man began to work for them, and went every morning to buy them food. Sometimes he felt like going into the forbidden room and often asked why he could not, but the old man always said,

'I could tell you, but it would do you no good. If you knew, it would bring you sorrow.'

One by one these old men died, and our friend would see to the funerals, while the others went on weeping and wailing.

The last to die was the one who had hired him, and his dying words were,

'Don't open that door.'

He buried the old man, and then there he was, alone in the house. Now he was very rich, but he was eaten up with curiosity and one day he could stand it no longer and he opened the forbidden door.

At once he found himself in the most glorious country, standing on the shore of an unknown sea. There was a little golden ship floating there, and some very pretty young women came out of it, welcomed him kindly, and pointing to the throne set up in the middle of the ship, they said, 'Take your seat, O King!'

And so he sailed over the waves seated on a golden throne, and came ashore by a palace in which a queen of the greatest beauty had been waiting and waiting for the husband who would come to her through the marvellous door. Three old and respectable women came forward:

'We are the three *cadis* of the town and we are here to celebrate your marriage with the queen. You will have nothing you need do. You are in a kingdom in which it is the women who work, who govern and who go to war. Men do nothing but plough and sow.'

That is how he became king of the blessed land where men need do nothing but plough and sow.

He was immensely happy. His every wish was fulfilled. He felt that he was living in a most beautiful dream. And he had nothing to do but enjoy this wonderful life, stroll in the fairy-tale gardens, and listen to songs so sweet that the birds in the sky stopped still. The queen, his exquisite wife whom he dearly loved, freed him from all the anxieties of power. For in that country women did everything, men only had to plough and sow.

After seven years of pure happiness, the queen said,

'Every seven years we have to fight against neighbours who come and attack us, and I must go and lead my army. Here are the keys of all the rooms in the palace. You can open them all, see and use everything in them. But this room here, I advise you not to open it, it would bring you sorrow.'

He promised not to do so, said goodbye to his darling wife and watched her go off at the head of her army of women.

'If opening the first door,' he said to himself when he was alone, 'brought me to this paradise, what wouldn't I find behind this one? I'll open it at once.'

As he was speaking, he put the key in the lock. No sooner did the doors swing open than a vulture swooped down, gripped him in its talons and took him back to the very place where he had opened the first door.

He lay senseless for a whole day. Then he came to himself, went into one of the rooms, and began to weep and wail.

The Story of Bartal and Jerâda

There was once a very poor couple. He was called Bartal, Little Sparrow, and she was Jerâda, Grasshopper. As they couldn't earn any money in their home town, they went to live in the sultan's city, first of all taking their little daughter to stay with an old cousin. Bartal began work as a soothsayer and Jerâda as a laundrymaid in the sultan's palace.

One day a silk scarf disappeared from where it was drying in the meadow. A calf had eaten it. Jerâda saw it all, but said nothing and let the search go on. When the sultan was told about it, he summoned all the women and told them:

'I want no thieves in my palace!'

Then Jerâda spoke up:

'I know a soothsayer who's so clever, he'll tell you at once who stole the scarf.' So they sent for him, and it was Bartal. On the way Jerâda told him what had happened.

Reaching the sultan's palace, the soothsayer sat down on the ground, took his sheep's shoulder-blade and his pen, made marks and dots on the blade and joined them up with little lines. Then with an air of inspiration he announced,

'O sultan, the scarf has not been stolen. A calf has eaten it.'

The calves were driven in, and the false soothsayer exclaimed, 'There's the calf!'

The sultan had it slaughtered at once and there indeed in its stomach they found the lost scarf. The astonished sultan gave Bartal a big handful of gold.

The vizier was watching, and he was jealous.

'This man's an impostor!' he exclaimed, and the sultan decided to test the man once more. At that moment a sparrow, a *bartal*, perched on the

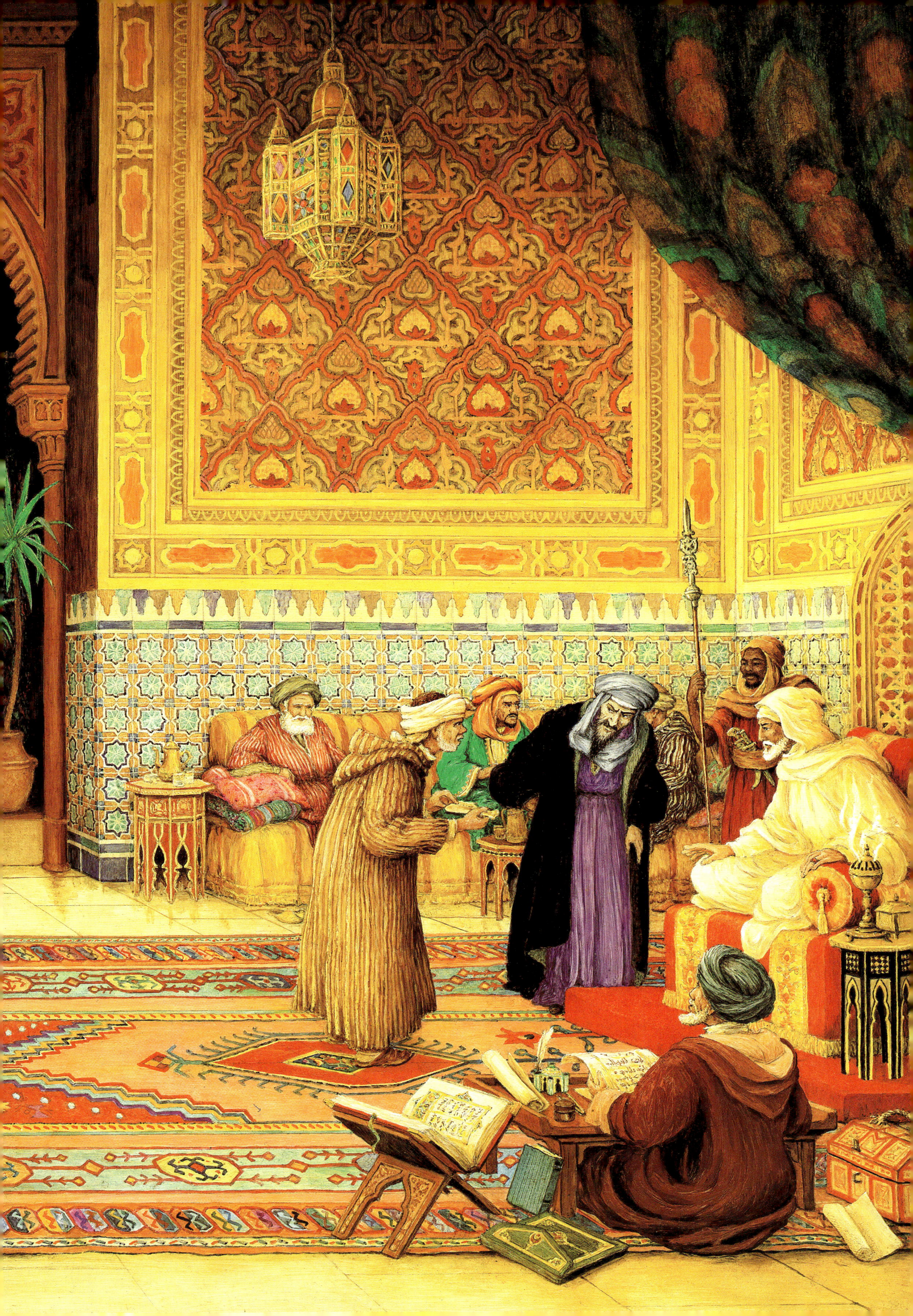

sultan's shoulder, and a grasshopper, *jerâda*, jumped onto his knee.

The sultan folded these two tiny creatures in his cloak, sent for Bartal and told him,

'I've got two little creatures hidden in my cloak; tell me what they are. If you can't do it, I shall kill you'

Utterly confused, Bartal replied,

'What can you be asking, you who command Bartal and Jerâda?' He gave his own and his wife's name, and all he meant was that he did not know.

And the sultan, hearing the names of the hidden creatures, was delighted. He lavished presents on Bartal and gave him a house and a daily income.

But Bartal was not happy. All the time he shook with fear in case someone came to fetch him to guess something impossible. So one day he wrote the sultan a letter, a letter with only one sentence, and it was this;

'He who works for the Sultan must do nothing without first counting the cost.' He left the letter in the house, shut the door, and set off with his wife for their own country.

A few days later the sultan sent for him, but there was no one there, nothing but the letter. It was brought to the sultan, who read it and thought it so good that he copied it out in his finest handwriting and set it up over his door so that everyone who came in could read it. He often thought about Bartal.

As for the vizier, he had got very rich working for his master, and now all he wanted was to be rid of him and take his place. He went to a smith, had a very sharp razor made, and coated it with a strong poison. Then on the day when the sultan's barber came to shave him, he summoned the barber and said,

'Barber, you know that the sultan is very displeased because your razors are dirty and they smell bad. Here is a new razor he has told me to give you, shave him with this.'

The barber took the razor and went to the sultan. But as he waited outside the door he read Bartal's sentence and thought, 'Yes, that makes sense. I don't understand all this stuff about razors, and I won't use the new one on the sultan unless he tells me to himself.' He spread his razors out on the floor, took one of his own and got ready to shave the sultan, who did not say anything. Then he shaved him as usual.

When he had finished, the sultan noticed the new razor beside the old ones and was surprised.

'Ah,' he said, 'you've got a new razor?'

'It's the one you gave the vizier to give me, so that I could shave you with it,'

'I gave the vizier nothing!' said the sultan, and he understood the dreadful truth. He called a slave girl, told her to fetch a young cat, and gave it to the barber, saying, 'Use your new razor on this little cat.' The blade had barely touched the animal when it fell dead. Then, mad with rage, the sultan sent for his vizier.

He was in his own room waiting for the wailing that would tell him the sultan was dead. When they told him that his master had been shaved and wanted to see him, he knew his plan had failed. In great anxiety he appeared before his master. The sultan welcomed him with a smile and kind words just as usual, then said to the barber,

'I would like you to shave the vizier with your new razor'.

The vizier trembled and he was dead even before the barber had finished shaving him.

Then the sultan said to the barber,

'You are my vizier. But I want to know why you did not use the new razor.?'

The new vizier replied,

'Because, Master, the writing over your door made me think.'

Let's go back to Bartal and Jerada

Back in their own country they had found their daughter, who was now a very beautiful young woman. A rich merchant came to ask her hand in marriage. Bartal said,

'I accept this marriage on condition that you pay me a hundred gold pieces every day while my daughter is living under your roof.'

The merchant was in love, he had a deed drawn up before the *cadi* agreeing to pay out these hundred pieces every day, and the wedding was celebrated. But then came the day when his money had all gone.

'We are going to leave this country,' he told his wife. 'That way I shan't have to pay your father any more.'

They came to the sultan's town. The merchant could find no work, but he got the sultan's foreman to take him on as a labourer.

Now the new vizier and the sultan used to visit the royal workshops every day. Watching Bartal's son-in-law as he toiled, the sultan exclaimed,

'That's a keen workman!' And the vizier answered,

'He must have a pretty wife to feed!'

Instantly the sultan wanted to see this wife. He ordered his faithful servant woman to follow the labourer, and she soon brought him such a description of the wife that he lost all common sense and went to the house while the husband was out at work.

At first the young woman refused to let him in. Then he told her that he was the sultan, and she opened the door. Dazzled by her great beauty, he fell in love with her at once. But the young woman dearly loved her husband, and when the sultan told her he wanted to marry her, she said,

'It is impossible, my lord, because the master cannot drink from the same water as the dog.'

The sultan realised how wrong he had been. He gave the young woman beautiful gifts and went back to the palace. Then he summoned the labourer and said,

'I did you wrong today, because I saw your wife and wanted to marry her. Now I must tell you that she is the most virtuous of women and she refused me. Don't leave her alone any more, go home and live happily with her.' And he lavished wealth upon him.

Bartal's son-in-law and his wife could now return to her parents and tell them their story.

Then Bartal said,

'This sultan had already made me rich and I didn't need your payments. I asked for them because I wanted to ruin you and make you poor, and then you would value my daughter! Now I give you back your money, I have kept it aside for you. Jerâda and I are returning to the sultan, who is a good and generous man.'

As soon as he got there, Bartal hurried to the sultan, who exclaimed,

'There you are, I was waiting for you! Sixty-six thousand welcomes! You must never go away again, you shall be my companion at table and in all delights, for it was the sentence you wrote that saved my life.'

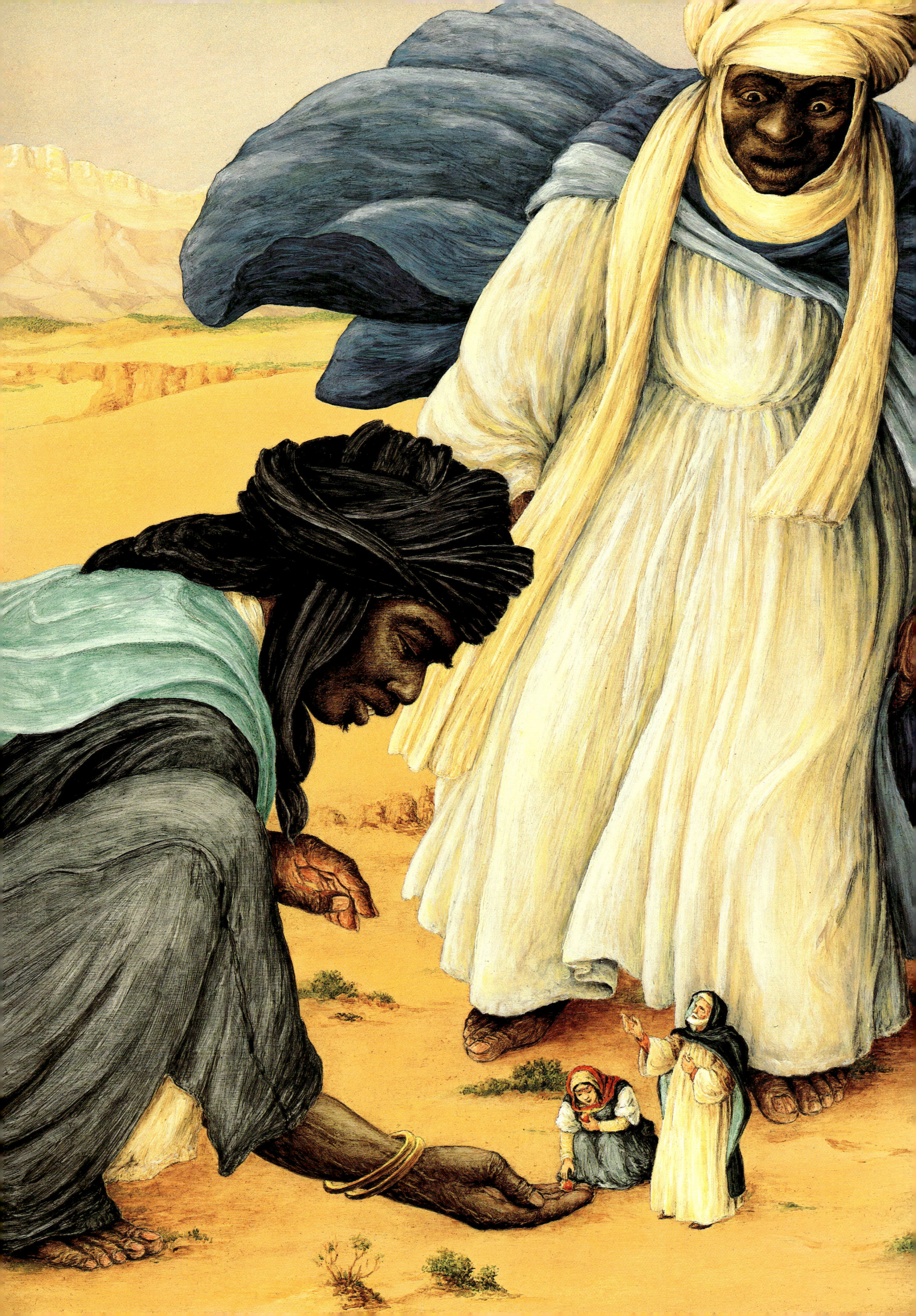

The Language of the Birds

There was a rich merchant in Fez who was sad because he had no children. He thought he was too old, and yet when he consulted a magician friend, he was told:

'You will have a son.' In fact the magician knew of a tree in a far-off land whose fruit would make those who ate it able to have children.

He twisted the ring of wisdom on his finger and there appeared two colossal black mighty *djinns* whose feet stood on the earth and whose heads touched the sky.

At the magician's command, they went to gather the fruit of the magic tree and brought it back to the merchant and his wife, who each ate two pieces.

Nine months later a fine boy was born, and his father gave him an excellent education in the best koranic school in the city.

When the boy was ten, the merchant took him with him on pilgrimage to Mecca. As they were visiting a town in Egypt on the way, they passed by a strange school, and through the delicately carved *moucharabiehs* they heard the students speaking in an unknown tongue.

'I am teaching my students the language of the birds,' said the schoolmaster with pride when the travellers asked him what it was.

The merchant liked the sound of this unusual knowledge, and he wanted his son to learn everything he could, so he left the boy with the old teacher and gave him seven small sacks of gold to pay for his instruction until he had completed his pilgrimage, and would pick the boy up on his way home to Fez.

But two years went by and the father did not return. He never could find the town and the school again and he went back home without his son.

'He fell into the sea,' he said to his wife, who cried till she was almost blind.

For ten years the merchant thought of nothing but his business. Self-centred and careless, he forgot his son, telling himself he would go and look for him when he needed him. Then one day he set off again on pilgrimage. Luckier this time, he found the town again, the street and the school. He heard again the 'tiu tiu tiu kiwit kiwit.' But he did not recognise the teacher. Instead of the old man there was a handsome young twenty-year old taking the class. He asked the young man about it. The master was ill, and had got his best pupil to stand in for him. The schoolmaster was sent for.

'You don't know your own son,' he said, pointing to the young teacher. 'He's a fine scholar, he can take my place now.'

Father and son then took ship for home. Out at sea, three birds came and perched on the rails and began to sing.

'What are they saying?' asked the father.

But the son would not answer.

'Tchi tchi tchi tiu tiu tiu,' cried the birds.

'Why won't you tell me?' insisted the father. Reluctantly the young man said,

'You really want to know? Well then, Father, they're saying that I shall become a sultan and one day you'll be a porter.'

The old merchant did not like this at all, and he chewed over his anger in silence.

Night fell, and he went down into the hold, emptied out all the goods from one of the chests, and put his sleeping son into it instead. He closed the lid carefully and threw the whole thing overboard.

And the ship sailed on towards the

Fortunate Empire.

Reaching the town of Moulay Idriss, the old merchant found his house burnt to the ground. It took him several days to find his wife, who had had to become a washerwoman to earn her living. After dragging on wretchedly for a while, the two old people decided to leave their native town and go and seek their fortune elsewhere.

Meanwhile a poor fisherman in a town on the coast was in a very bad mood because he had been fishing since daybreak and could catch nothing in his net. He had just come ashore in despair and was sitting on the sand with his head in his hands. Glancing up, he saw a large chest tossing on the waves and drifting towards the shore. Quickly he put out again, caught hold of the wreckage, and took it home. When he and his wife managed to open it, they saw a handsome young man in fine clothing.

'Man or *djinn*?' they cried in terror.

'I'm a man of flesh and blood,' said the young man. 'Don't be afraid!' They gave him good hot soup and did all they could for him, and he told them,

'You are my only parents now. Here's the money I've got in my purse, take it. And sell these fine clothes, I've no use for them.'

This young man, born as we know in a strange way, and brought up in unusual conditions, had the gift of bringing happiness with him. From the day he came to the fisherman's house, the fish swam into his nets and joy reigned under his roof. And he was well educated and liked to visit the schools and mosques. He also became a close friend of the *cadi's* son.

Now the sultan of this town had a problem. For some time now, every day as he was sitting among all the people of the palace, three birds would fly around him, would cheep and twitter as if asking him a question. Then, oh abomination, they did their business on the sultan's head and flew away.

The sultan had offered half his kingdom to the man could free him from this calamity. Anyone who tried and failed would die. Several had already had their heads cut off. As the *cadi* was said to be a very learned man, the sultan sent for him and gave him a week in which to make arrangements.

The unhappy *cadi* went home, set his affairs in order as if for death, and explained matters to his son.

That evening the fisherman's adopted son met his friend the *cadi's* son, saw how sad he was, asked the reason, and discovered what a fate was awaiting his father.

'Is that all?' he exclaimed. 'Don't you worry any more. I'll sort it out for you. No point waiting a week. Tell your father to go to the sultan tomorrow, and I'll go with him.'

The young man went to the palace with the *cadi*, bowed to the sultan three times, and asked him if he would give him half his kingdom if he succeeded. The three birds were there already and had started twittering.

'I accept,' replied the sultan.

'Fetch the lawyers in to register the gift,' said the young man prudently, and as soon as this was done, he began to talk with the birds. And there it was, baffling, Tiu tiu tiu kiwit kiwit tchi tchi tiu tiu.

'They are asking you for justice,' he said at last, turning to the king. 'They are two males and a female, the one on the left is from the east, the other from the west. The female belonged to this western one, who was away on a journey a long time. Thinking he was dead, she married the other and lived with him a year. They want the sultan to settle it for them.'

The sultan had no idea what to say.

'If you wish, Emir of all Believers, I will give

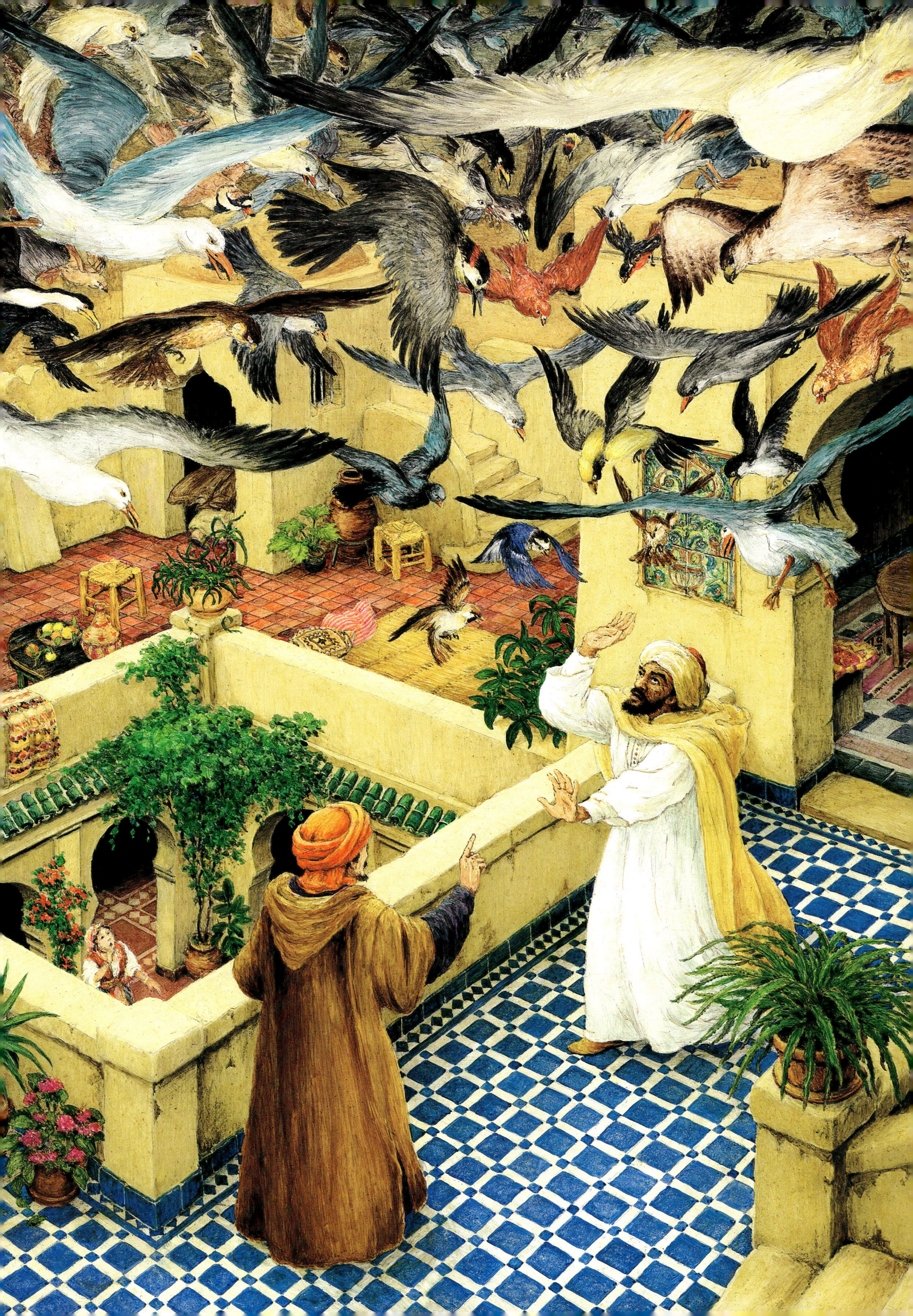

judgment in your place, and everything will be all right.' The sultan agreed, and the young man said to the bird from the east,

'Go east.'

To the bird from the west he said,'

'Go west.'

And to the hen bird he said,

'Follow the one you love.'

Both male birds flew off as commanded, and the hen bird unhesitatingly followed her first husband towards the west.

Everyone was amazed. But the sultan was already wishing he had not given away half his kingdom for the sake of a few tiutiutius, and it looked as if he was not going to keep his word. Then the young man threatened to call all the birds in the world together so that they could do as the first three had done.

Indeed he called out several times in bird language and suddenly the sultan saw the whole sky darken above his head. All the birds of all the species of all the countries in all the world had gathered above the imperial court. It made a fine tiutiutiu concert. And the young man said,

'I shall order them all to do their business on you if you don't keep your promise.'

The sultan had to give in; the birds went away. His bad temper did not last long because the young man was so pleasant and so attractive that he could not help liking him. He sent for the fisherman and his wife, who put on royal robes and gave thanks to heaven for their child of fortune. One week later the old sultan died, leaving the young man as his sole heir.

Meanwhile his real parents after many journeys arrived in this town.

'Try to get taken on as a porter,' advised the old woman. 'I'll get work as a washerwoman. We'll meet this evening.'

That very day the sultan ordered his people to bring wood into the palace for the winter. And the steward hired some porters to do this. That is how the father became a porter, just as the birds had said, in the city where his son was sultan. Leaning on the terrace, the son recognised his father. He resented his having thrown him into the sea, indeed he did, but he had too noble a heart to wish for vengeance. He ordered his men to fetch the porter and take him indoors. He began to question him:

'Have you a family, a son, a wife?' for he wanted news of his mother.

'I've never had a son,' said the old man, whose conscience was not easy on this point. 'But I have a wife, very old, very shaky, she's a washerwoman.'

'Go and fetch her,' the sultan ordered two of his servants.

Thus they were all reunited.

'Poor woman!' said the sultan in distress. 'What unhappiness has brought you to this state?'

'Ah, Lord, my husband caused me great sorrow. He lost our son.'

'Would you recognise him?'

'Oh yes, Lord! He has a beauty spot on his right shoulder.' At once the sultan stripped off, showed his naked arm and embraced his mother, who wept with joy.

He forgave his father, and ordered his servants to bathe him and his wife in the *hammam* and to dress them both in royal robes.

Then he lived with his real parents and his adoptive parents, reigned for many years and brought joy to his subjects.

The Woman and the Cadi

One day a man bought a measure of wheat. He took it home and said to his wife, 'Grind this wheat.' But his wife refused. Then the man went to complain to the *cadi*, who said,

'Send your wife to me and I'll give her a talking to!'

She went, and he gave her a stinging rebuke.

'A wife has to grind the wheat and never send it to the mill, where the miller will steal half of it. So go and grind your wheat!'

At that moment the woman happened accidentally to move her veil aside. She quickly put it back, but the *cadi* saw that she was very pretty. He got up, came close to her and said,

'I shall come and see you tomorrow.'

Next day he arrived, but he had only just gone in when someone knocked on the door.

'It's my husband!' cried the woman. 'Quick, take your things off, wrap yourself in this coverlet, sit down at the handmill. You grind the wheat and I'll tell him you're a girlfriend who's come to help me.'

Quickly the *cadi* stripped off, wrapped himself in the coverlet and began turning the mill as the husband came in. But the wife, instead of getting rid of her husband, used every device she could think of to keep him there all afternoon. The *cadi* turned and turned the mill until by evening he had ground all the wheat and his shoulder was in agony. The husband went out, the furious *cadi* put on his own clothes and went away too.

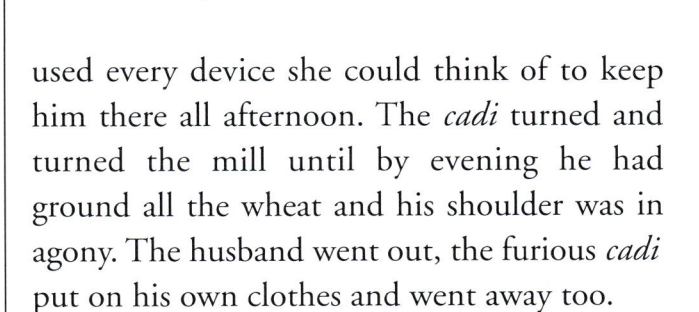

A few days later the husband bought some more wheat and gave it to his wife. Again she refused to grind it. Again he went to complain to the *cadi*, taking his wife with him.

He made his complaint, but before he had finished his wife cried out,

'Oh cadi, you know how much grinding hurts, tell this man to take his wheat to the mill!' And the judge remembered, and had to agree with her. He sent them away, the husband furious with his decision and the wife delighted.

The Stolen Treasure

A woman had a son, Amesmar, and a daughter, Tamesmart. They were very poor and often did not have enough to eat. One day Amesmar said to his sister,

'Let's go to the palace and rob the king!' Off they went, made a hole in the wall of the treasure chamber, and stole all the gold they could carry. They went back again a few days later, and in this way they were able to build themselves a fine house, buy cattle and live in perfect happiness.

One day when the king needed money he went down into the treasure chamber and discovered the theft. Next day he announced in the council meeting before all his ministers and courtiers that his treasury had been robbed.

'I will give my daughter to the man who catches the thief,' he said. 'What's more I will build him a castle and will heap such wealth on him that he and his children shall live happily all their days!'

No one could find the thief. An old merchant went to the palace, prostrated himself before the king and said,

'I can tell you how to catch him.'

'How?' asked the king.

'Put a cubit's depth of pitch into each of two tall man-sized jars, then move the treasure to a new place. The thief will think it must be in these jars, will get into one, he will stick in the pitch and you will have him.'

'Go home,' said the king, 'and I'll try out your trap.' The king then had two jars put in the treasure chamber, poured a cubit's depth of pitch into each one, went out and locked the door.

Not long afterwards Amesmar said to his sister,

'Suppose we go and rob the king again?'

They got into the treasure chamber just as they had done before, and could not find the money where it used to be. But they saw the two jars standing against the wall.

'I think,' said the boy, 'it must be in there.'

'Help me down,' said Tamesmart, 'I'll find out.' Amesmar lowered her into the jar and let her go when she was almost at the bottom.

'Pull me up! I don't know what I've got into, but I'm in it right up to my knees!'

She reached her hands up to him and he tried to pull her out, but he couldn't do it.

'Sister, this is very awkward! If I leave you, they'll find you tomorrow morning, they'll question you and know where to find me. The soldiers will arrest me and we shall both have our heads cut off. I'd better cut yours off myself, that way at least I'll save my own.'

He cut her head off and took it away so that the king would not be able to identify the body.

Next day when the king went into the treasure chamber he found a headless corpse stuck in the jar. He had it brought out and ordered it to be displayed in the place where he held audience

'Who can identify this body?' he asked the assembled meeting.

'Lord,' they all said at once, 'no one can identify a body without a head!'

'Then let it be taken out of the town and set up in the middle of the road. The relatives will come and mourn over it; arrest them and bring them to me, men or women.'

Meanwhile Amesmar had told his mother about the great sorrow that had struck them, and gave her his sister's head. She cried all day and all night and then said,

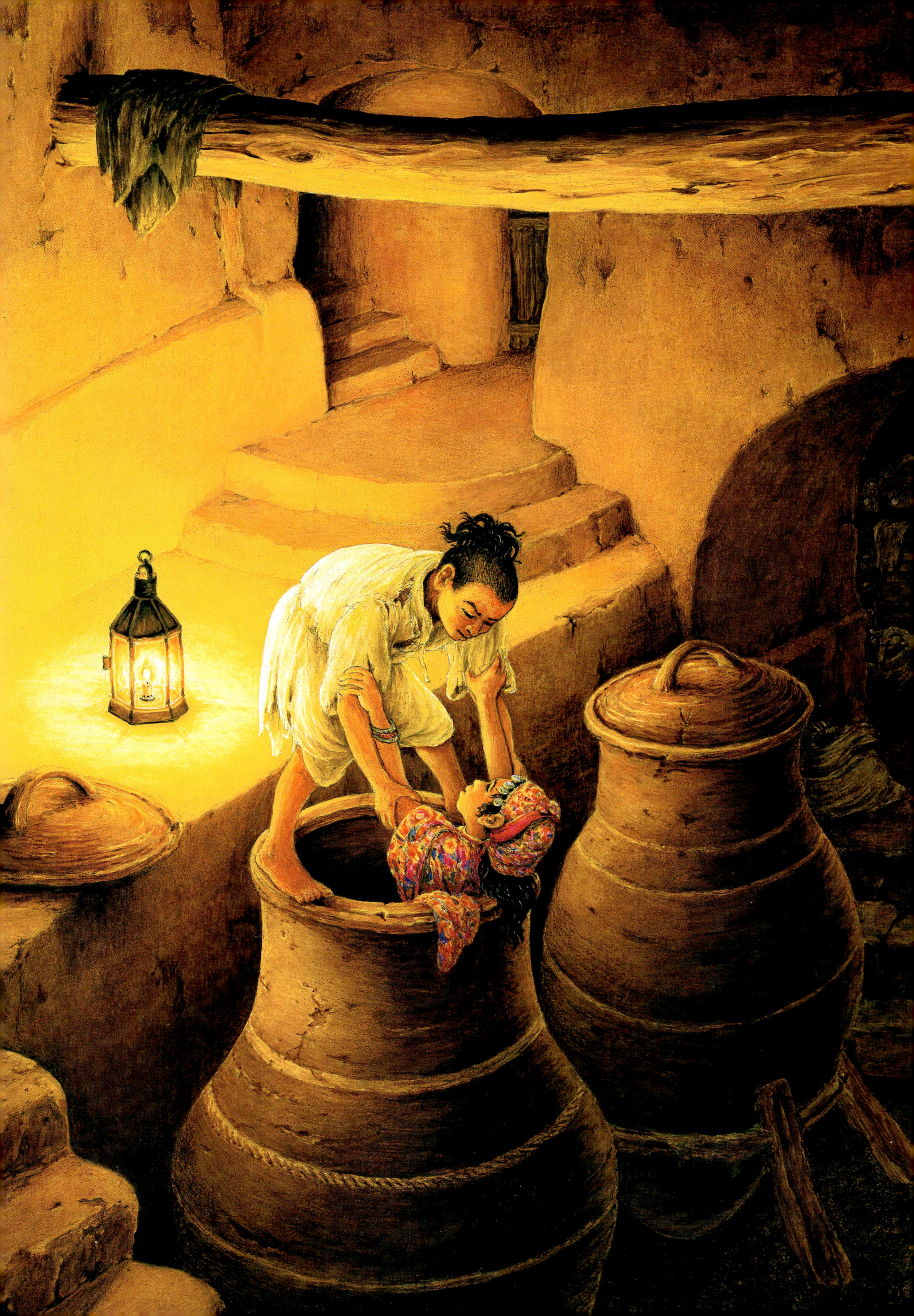

'You must take me to her body.' Amesmar was doubtful about that. He was afraid she would not be able to help crying, and people would see her and arrest them both. Then he had a clever idea. He went to the market, bought an unruly mule and some jars and pots, put these into a net and loaded it onto the mule. Then he went towards the town, with his mother following him. When they came near the body, he excited the mule, which danced and lashed about until the net and all the pots and jars fell down with a great crash. His mother crouched over her daughter's body, wailing and weeping. The guards, who thought she was crying about the cooking pots, left her alone. Then, worn out but relieved by her tears, the unhappy mother went home.

Soon afterwards she said to her son,

'Now we must find a way to steal your sister's body from them.' But it was watched night and day by the royal guards. How could they manage?

What was to be done? Amesmar collected a flock of goats, fixed two candles to each one's horns and drove them towards the town. Not far from his sister's body he lit the candles, and the glittering flock moved forward into the dark. At this sight the terrified guards fled in all directions. Amesmar was then able to take up his sister's corpse and bring it to his mother.

'Here is your daughter's body,' he said. And in the morning they buried it.

Another night Amesmar decided to slip into the palace to find the king and punish him for having caused his sister's death. A door blocked his way, but he pulled it down, so did a second, and then a third; he pulled them both down and reached the sleeping king. He flung himself at him and rained blows on him, finishing with a blow behind the ear, which knocked him right out. With the king well and truly punished, Amesmar went home. The king came to his senses at daybreak but had to stay in his bedroom all day and did not hold audience till the following day.

He said to the ministers and nobles all around him,

'Summon my people to a general assembly.'

Criers were sent to every market place. Amesmar learned in this way what the king meant to do. He changed from his fine clothes into rags and went and sat in the mosque. The king spoke to the assembled crowd:

'To the man who can guess what happened to me the day before yesterday at dinner, I will give my daughter in marriage. I will also build him a palace and I will lavish such wealth upon him that he shall live in joy, he, his children and his grandchildren!'

No one gave him the answer he was waiting for.

'Is there no one else to be heard?' asked the king.

'Lord, everyone has spoken except for a wretch sheltering in the mosque; he is warming himself at the fire, his clothes are such rags!'

'Bring him.'

The soldiers went to fetch him. The king asked him the question.

'I will not answer, Lord, unless you grant me forgiveness before God!'

'Granted, all shall be forgiven. Speak!'

'It was I, Lord, who pulled down the three doors of your palace, who got into your room as you slept, I who struck you and gave you the blow behind your ear which knocked you out.'

The king had to keep his promise. He gave his daughter to Amesmar, he had a castle built for him and lavished gold upon him. Amesmar did not forget his mother, he installed her in the castle the king had given him. And the wedding celebrations were magnificent.

Wit is the Best Weapon

One evening four men met beside a road. They sat on their heels to talk of this and that. One of them tossed a challenge to the others:

'Everyone tell a ridiculous story. The first who says "You're lying!" gets a forfeit, he has to pay the rest a fine.'

'What fine?'

'A measure of toasted corn!'

All this being settled, they agreed to meet in the same place next day.

One of them started telling a story; another, finding it quite ridiculous, cried out,

'You're lying!'

'A forfeit!' shouted the others.

And so the game went on until they had all had to pay up except for one of them who was never caught out. The rest got together and agreed that next day they would all tell such impossible stories that he would have to end up saying, 'He's lying!'

They met as usual and one of them began:

'Yesterday,' he said, 'I saw something really amazing.'

'What did you see?'

'I saw builders at work between heaven and earth putting up a house with no foundations.'

They turned to their comrade and asked,

'What do you think of that?'

'Oh, it certainly must have been God,' said the man with a ready wit. 'He has decided to come nearer to men and is having a new house built.'

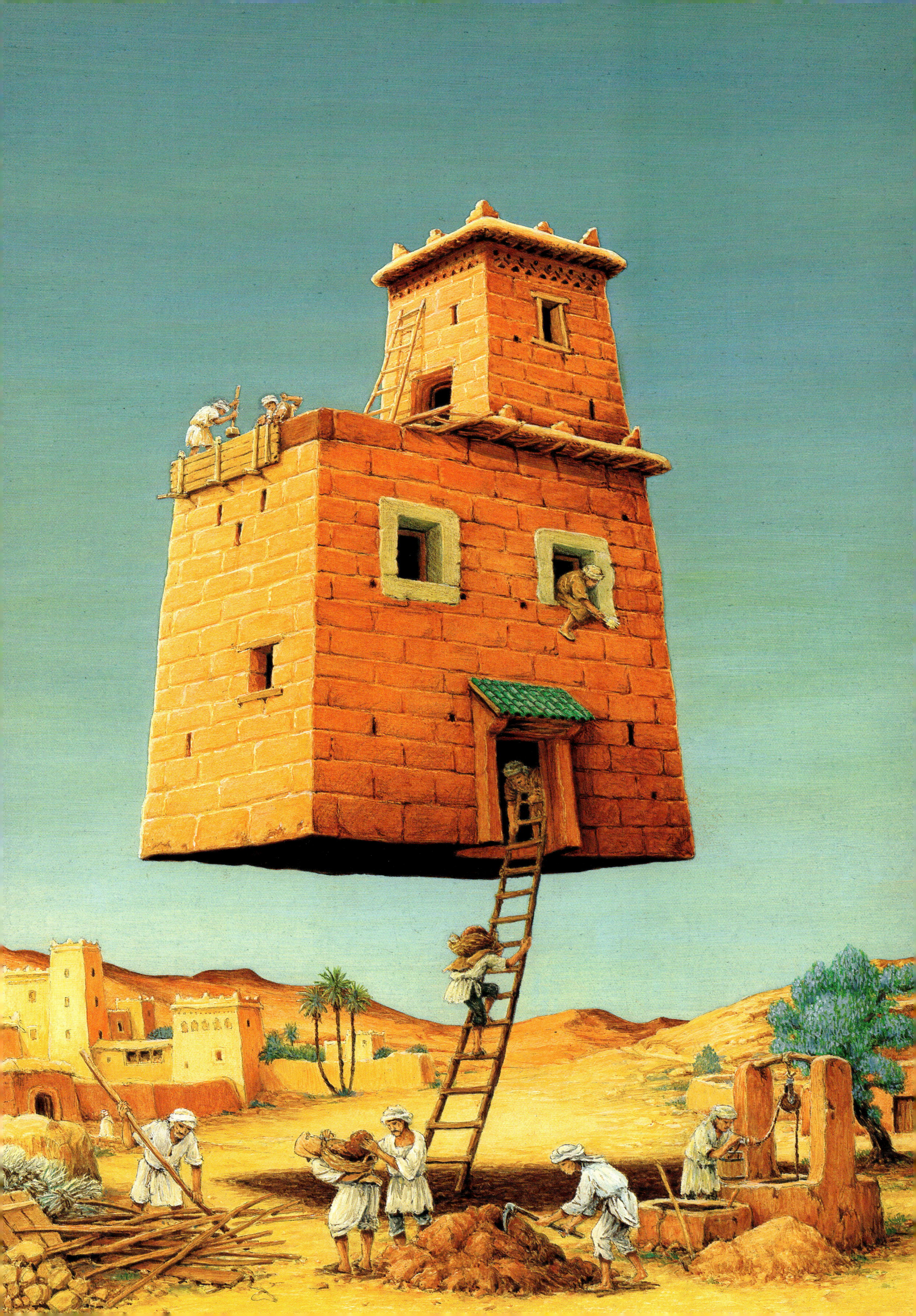

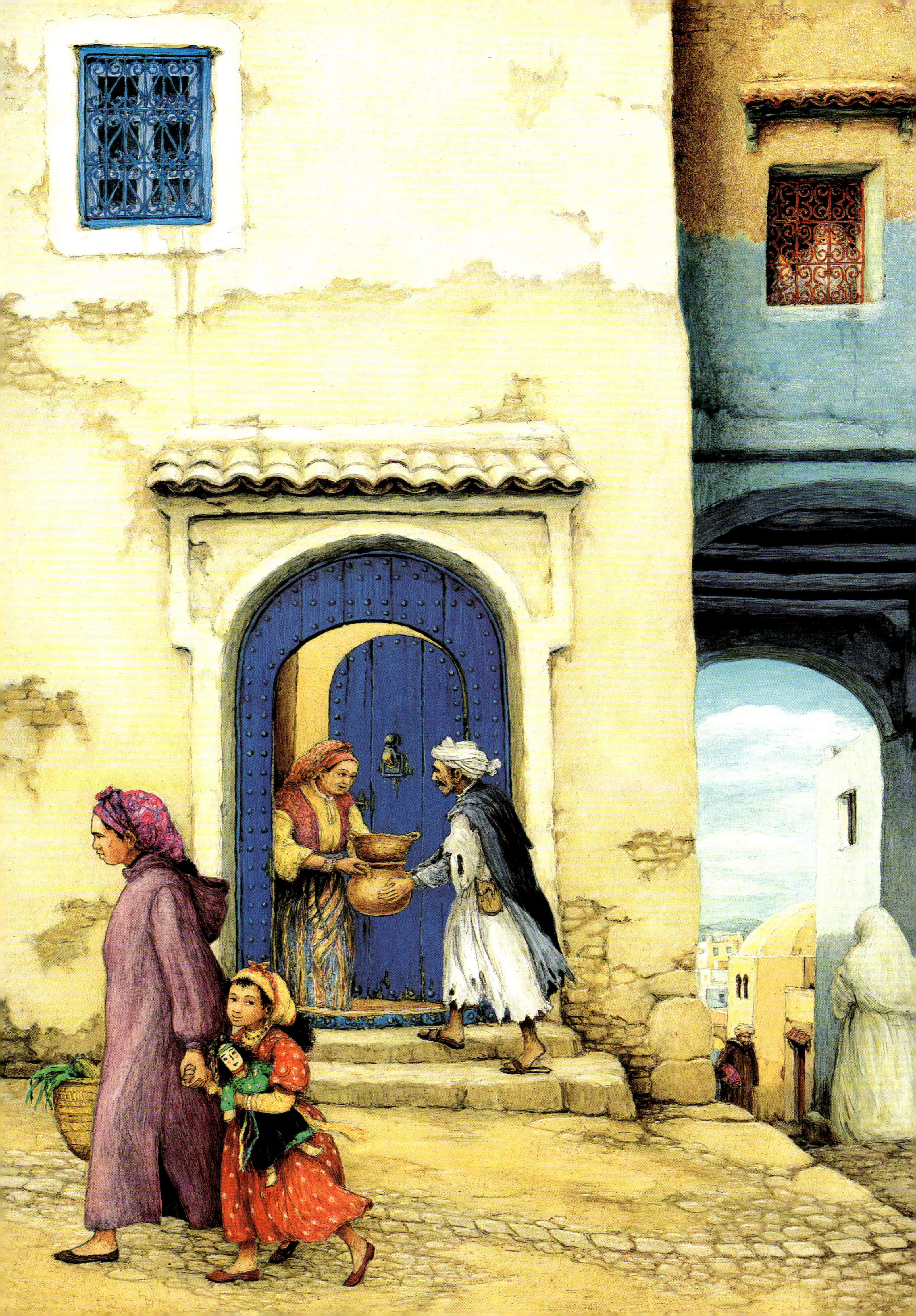

The Man with a Stupid Wife

One day a man went home and said to his wife,

'Here is some semolina. Make some couscous for Lent, Lent's on the way.'

She had finished doing this when she heard a noise in the alley-way - it was a thief. She went out, saw him and asked,

'Who are you?'

'I'm Lent,' he answered. 'He's come to get his food,' she thought, and immediately gave him the couscous.

When her husband came back she said to him,

'Lent came, and I gave him all of it.'

'What Lent? Lent doesn't start for another two months.' Then he realised that she had given all the couscous to a man whose name was Lent. Furiously he swore never to come home unless he found a woman more stupid than his wife. And off he went.

He came to another country where a woman asked him,

'Where are you from?'

'From the other world,' he answered. Then she said,

'You wouldn't have seen my son there, would you? He's dead, and perhaps you could give me news of him.'

'Oh yes,' he said, 'he's got no clothes and he needs a cloak and some money.'

The stupid woman went into her house, got a new cloak and some money, and handed it all over to the man, urging him to be sure and give it to her son in the other world. He went away at once and took the road home.

When this woman's husband came in, she told him that she had had news from the other world and had sent her son a cloak and some money. The husband was furious; he mounted his horse and set off after the man. He, when he saw a horseman galloping after him, knew at once what was happening. He was just crossing a field of ripe beans, so now he hid his bundle and began to pick beans.

Reaching him, the husband drew rein and called out,

'Master of the field, haven't you seen a man go by wearing such and such a cloak?'

'Oh yes,' he answered, 'and going fast. Cut across here and you'll catch him up. But don't go on the horse, he'll hear the sound of the hooves and hide.'

The husband gave him the horse to hold and went off along the short cut. The man mounted the horse and rode away fast. When he got home he told his wife,

'I've come back because I've found a woman even stupider than you.'

As for the husband of the second woman, the short cut did him no good, he couldn't find the man he was chasing. He went back to the bean field, where he found no horse and no 'master of the field'. Then, much ashamed, he went back to his own house, and said to his wife,

'Wife, you were right. People do come back from the other world. I found the man who came from it and told you about our son, and to help him get back faster, I've given him my horse as well.'

Fair Shares

A man went one day to a place on the river bank where flood water stayed and did not ebb away. He took off his shirt and made a sort of trap out of it, tying the ends with a palm leaf cord, weighted it with mud and sank it in the water. He left it there a while, then drew it up and found in it a live silvery fish with amazing colours that flashed from red to white to yellow. He took this wonderful fish to the king, hoping to be given a present which would relieve his poverty. At the first palace door the doorkeeper said,

'I'll let you in on condition you give me half of the present you get from the king.'

'Yes, of course,' he said.

The second doorkeeper said just the same. The he reached the vizier, who also said the same. At last he reached the king and gave him the fish.

'What do you want?' the king asked him.

'Lord, the grace of one thousand strokes with a rod.'

'Are you out of your mind? People usually ask for money!' But he granted him what he asked for.

'Lord,' added the man, 'send your servants with me until I leave the palace.'

These men went with him first of all to the vizier, who made a sign to him and said softly,

'How much?'

'A thousand.'

'Give me five hundred!' Then the man turned to the servants and said,

'Stretch him out on the ground and give him five hundred strokes.'

Then they came to the doorkeeper and gave him two hundred and fifty strokes, then to the other one who got half of the remainder.

Next day the king attended his council meeting as usual. He did not see his vizier there, so sent for him.

'I am ill!' the vizier had the messenger informed.

'Ill or not, he is to come!' ordered the king. The vizier came, and told his story. The king sent for the fisherman.

'Whatever have you done?'

'Lord, I came in the hope of receiving a gift from you which would allow me and my children to live, but all I found around you were greedy people. That is why I asked you for the thousand strokes … and I shared them out.'

After a good long laugh, the king had a gift given to the fisherman.

A House Bought in Paradise

In the days when Moulay Abderrahmân was sultan, he had a friend who was very dear to him. He took him everywhere he went and could not do without him. In spite of this, the friend did not get rich. He had no garden, no house, no property of any kind. And if by any chance he was not staying with his master, he had to go and live in the military camp and he didn't much care for that. He would have liked a house of his own.

One day when the sultan had given him a purse of gold, he picked out one of the courtiers and said,

'Go to Fez and buy me a house.'

The courtier set off. As he was arriving outside the city walls he heard a poor woman who was begging by the roadside say,

'The man who gives me bread for my children will have a fine house after his death.'

The courtier tossed her the sultan's purse and turned home for Marrakech without even going into Fez.

Not long afterwards the sultan Moulay Abderrahmân gathered his troops together and, accompanied by his friend and the courtier, returned to Fez, his capital city. As soon as they arrived, the friend asked the courtier for the keys of his house.

'The house I bought you is in Paradise,' said the friend, 'and only God has the keys.'

'All right, let's go to the lawyer and get a deed of settlement.'

This they did, and the new proprietor put the deed into a strongbox and kept the key carefully.

Just before he died he said to the friends around him,

'You'll find a deed of ownership in my box. I want it buried with me, under my head.'

His friends faithfully carried out his last wish.

Some years went by. The courtier was walking in a graveyard one day, meditating, when he saw a letter addressed to himself lying at his feet. He picked it up and in no small surprise read,

'Friend, the house you bought for me is perfect in every way, and I am so grateful I have bought you one just the same.'

Princess Saktsa or Maskoutsa

A king had a daughter who was very lovely but very cruel. She had announced that she would only marry the man who could make her speak. Many had tried, had failed and according to custom had been executed and their heads set up on *Bâb Mahrouq*, then called Bab ech-chari'ah, the Gate of the Law.

The sultan of a neighbouring kingdom had seven sons. Knowing of the princess' reputation for beauty and for cruelty and fearing for his sons, he sent for them as he was dying. He gave each one of them an egg, as was the custom when something must not be forgotten, and advised them never for any reason to go over the mountain on the border of their domains and beyond which lay the neighbouring kingdom.

His eldest son succeeded him. Out hunting one day on the slopes of this mountain, curiosity overcame him and he went on and entered the neighbouring country. As he approached the capital, he saw ninety-three heads drying over the gateway. An old woman lived in a cave close by.

'Oh, aunt,' he said to her, 'why are all these heads here? Is the land at war?'

'No, my son, it is the cruel princess who causes so much sorrow.' And she told him how they had died.

But she could not stop the young king carrying out the plan that had sprung up in his mind. He gave her his horse to take care of, and a sack of gold, and decided to go and ask for the princess's hand.

In the evening after the sunset prayer he arrived at the palace dressed like a young

32

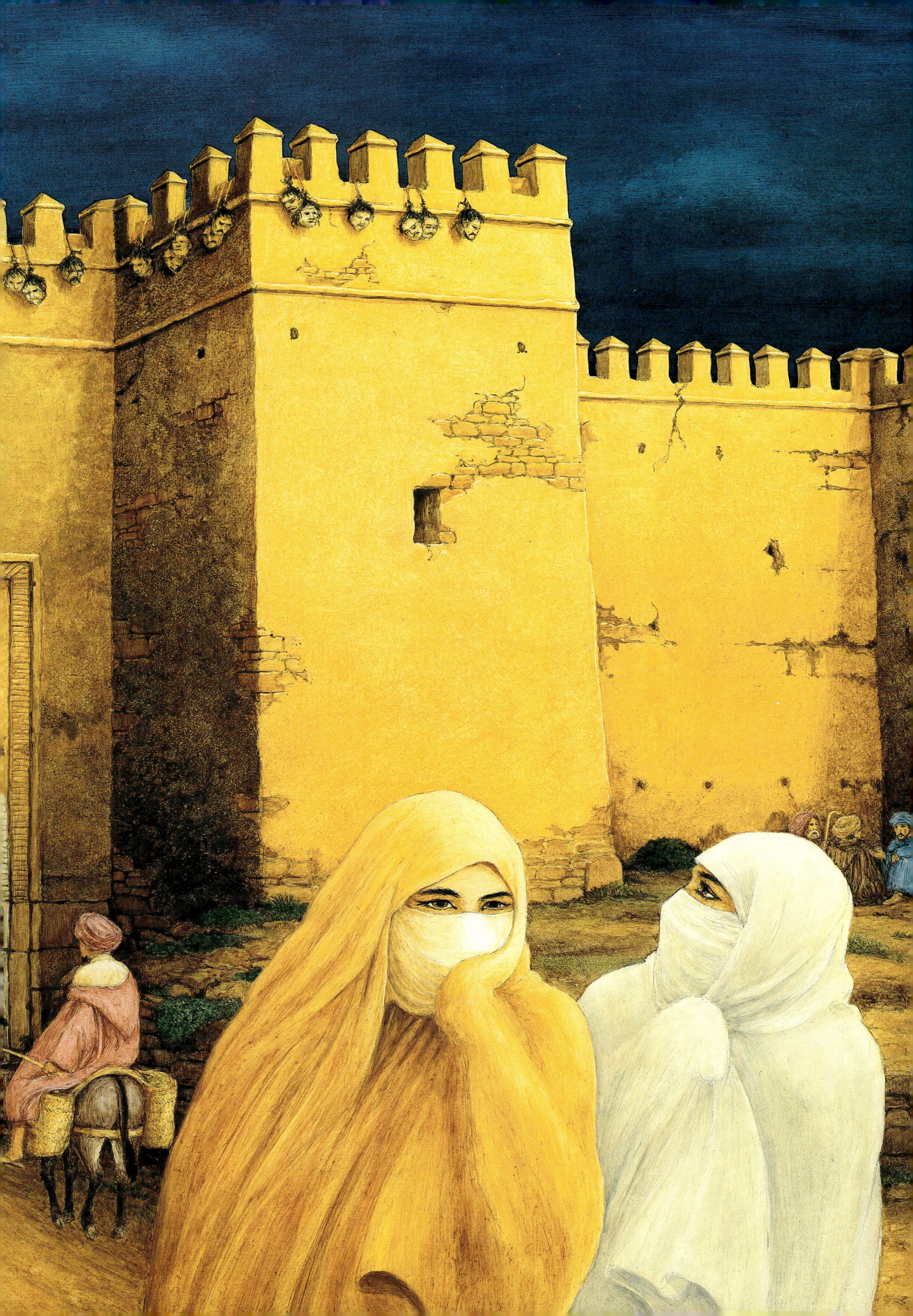

bridegroom on his wedding day. The women brought him in to undergo the test he must endure at the hands of Princess Saktsa, Silent, or Maskoutsa, Who Won't Speak. He had to pass through seven curtains, and at each one slaves perfumed him and said,

'Enter, young bridegroom!'

The test lasted all night long. Lawyers were present behind the wall hangings, ready to record the princess' consent. But the young man could not get her to unclench her teeth. They ate. They drank. He offered her tea, which she refused without a word. Dawn whitened the windows, the time of prayer came. The young prince was killed and his head was added to the ninety-three others on the dreadful gate.

His next brother followed him. He too climbed the mountain, reached the city, saw the heads, talked to the old woman in her cave and suffered the same fate as his elder. So did the others, and soon the old woman had six sacks of gold and six horses to take care of, while ninety-nine heads rotted on the city wall.

The last and youngest of the sons came in his turn, saw the heads of his six brothers and swore vengeance, although the old woman begged him to go away, explaining how they had all been punished for disobeying their father.

Then he asked for the princess' hand, accepted the terms, but requested six days' delay. The sultan agreed to this, and lodged him in a house with a pleasant *riad*. He spent his time meditating in this garden and playing his *guembri*, for he was a fine musician and skilled in all kinds of knowledge. Three doves often came and listened and greatly enjoyed his playing.

On the sixth day the doves began talking near him in Arabic. They were in fact *djinns*.

'Sisters, can't we do something for this young man who delights us with his music every evening?' said the first.

'Oh yes,' said the other two, 'but what can we do?'

'Tomorrow,' said the first dove, 'he must go into the princess' presence in silence, without a single word, so as to annoy and puzzle her. Then we three will come and bring a case before him, and he will deliver such a judgment on it that she won't be able to help contradicting him.'

The doves thoroughly understood the female heart. On the seventh evening the young prince went to the palace, passed through the seven curtains, made the tea, ate and drank in the princess' company without offering her a word, then began to play his *guembri*. Then the doves flew in, perched by the window and began to ask for justice. They were, they said, three sisters who disagreed about their father's inheritance. Instead of sharing it out equally, the eldest wanted to take three sixths, leaving two sixths for the second sister and only one for the youngest. The two other sisters did not agree at all. All three asked the young musician to settle this dispute.

'This is what must be done,' he said, and he pronounced in favour of the eldest dove, thus contradicting both custom and the law of the Koran.

Thoroughly shocked, the princess, who prided herself on her knowledge of the law, exclaimed,

'No, that is an appalling judgment!'

'She has spoken, she has spoken!' cried all those present, and the lawyers recorded her defeat and drew up the marriage contract.

And that is how the young sultan took beautiful Princess Saktsa or Maskoutsa home to his capital and married her.

Shrewd Tales

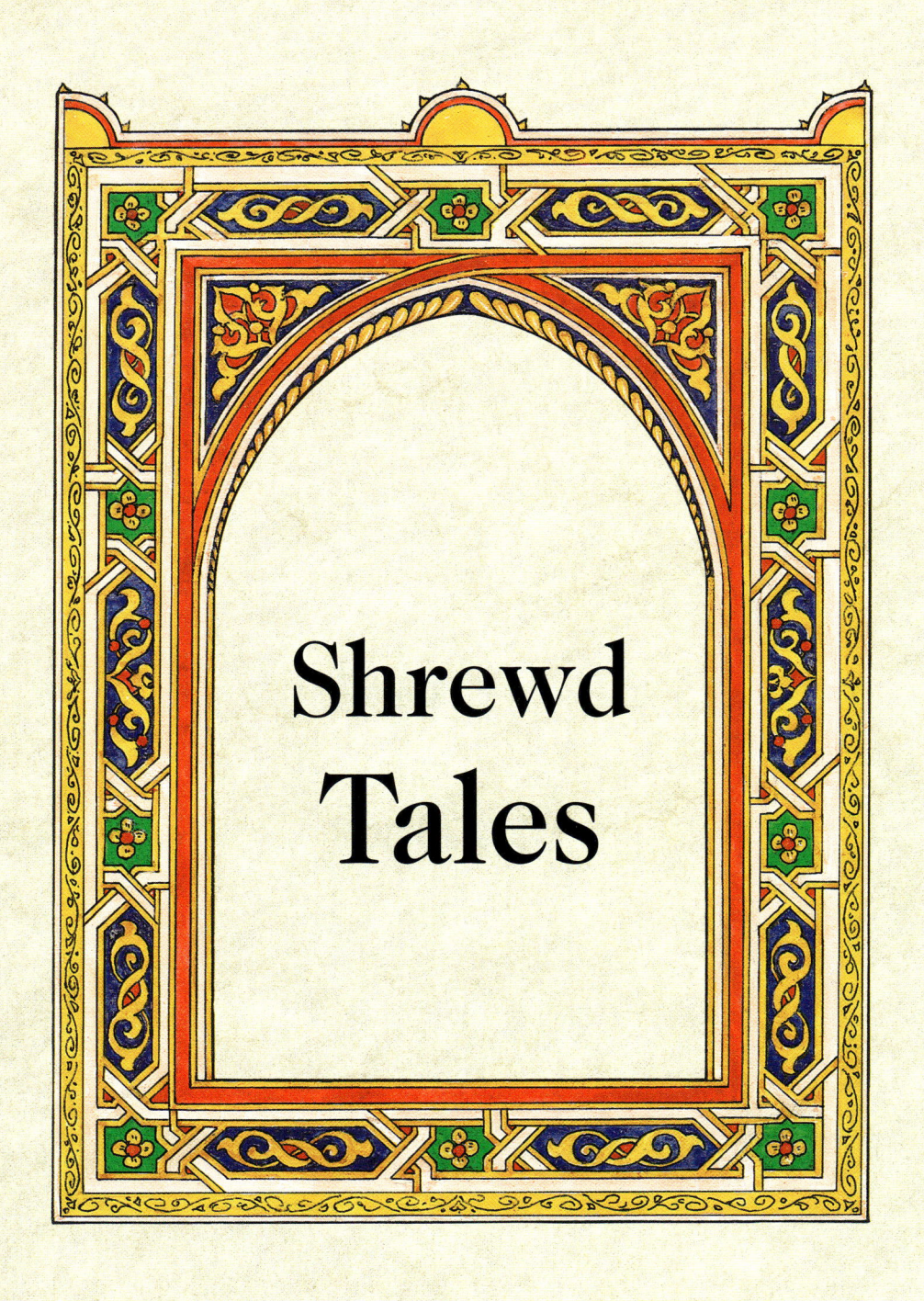

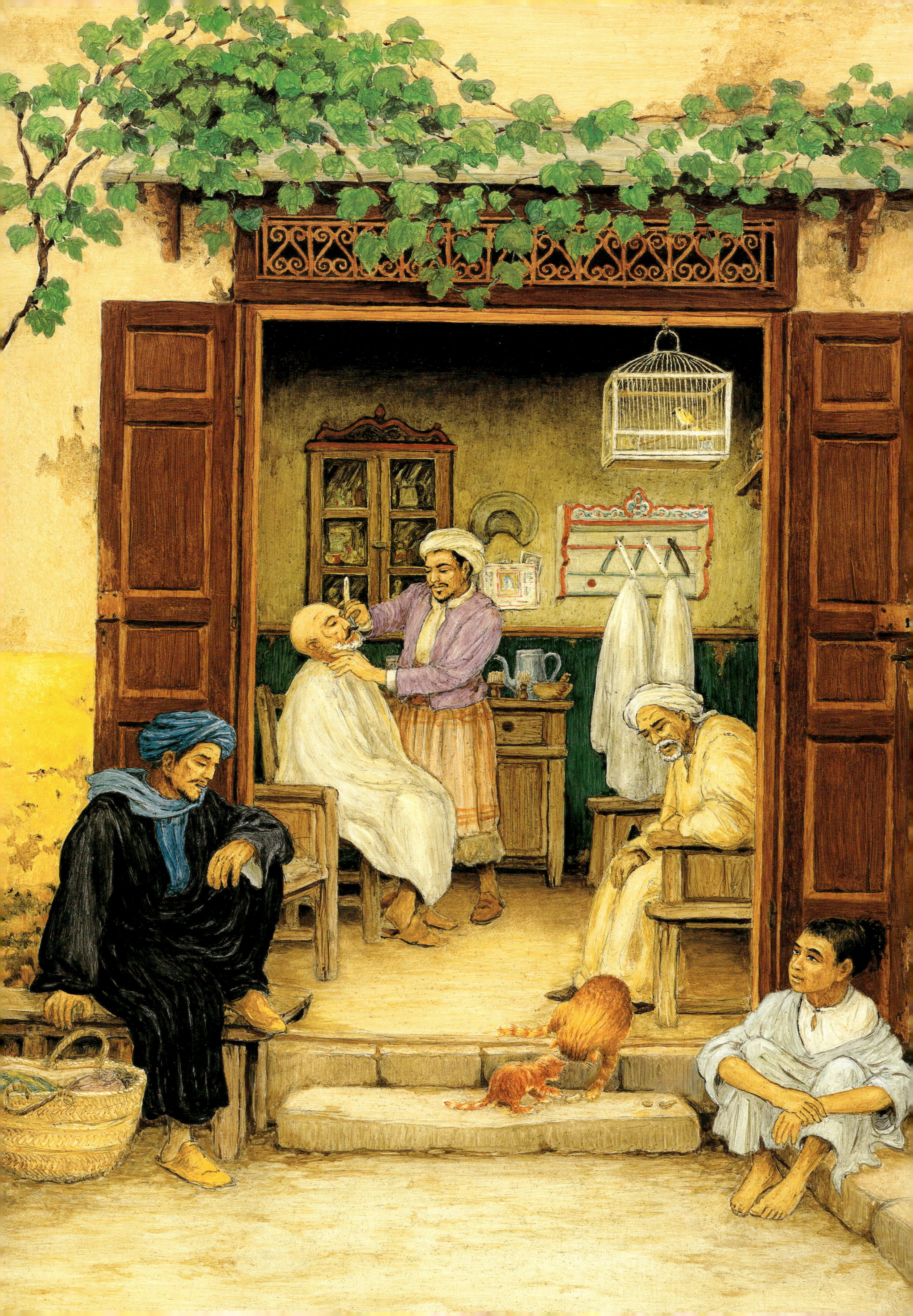

The Barber in Love

A barber was in love with his cousin and wanted to marry her. But the girl's godmother would not hear of it. The barber decided not to take any money from his customers until he and his cousin were married. When anyone went into his shop and tried to pay him, he would say,

'I despise money, all I want is human affection!' A foreigner came in one day, and as he was about to pay him, the barber stopped him, saying,

'I don't take money, all I care about is friendship.' The foreigner went home to his own country. A month or so later he returned to the barber's and again tried to pay and got the same response.

'But what has happened to you then, to make you despise money like this?' he asked. The barber explained that he loved his cousin, very much wanted to marry her, but that the girl's godmother persisted in refusing all his offers.

At once the foreigner went to a smithy, had a pair of pincers and a bludgeon made, then returned to the barber's and spent the first part of the night there. Then, when the barber had pointed out the cousin's house to him, he took the pincers and the bludgeon and climbed over the wall. He reached the courtyard and found the godmother asleep beside the girl. He nipped her nose with the pincers and tugged.

'Who's that?' she cried.

'It is I, the Angel of Death!' And he interrogated her as the Angel does a dead man who is passing his first night in limbo. 'Why do you keep refusing to let the barber marry his cousin?'

'I don't want to give her to him!'

All night long he tormented her and badgered her with questions, and as day broke he vanished.

He spent the next day with his friend the barber. At nightfall he climbed into the house again, went into the room where the obstinate godmother slept and pulled her nose with the pincers.

'What do you want with me?' she said as she woke.

'Give the girl to her cousin the barber!' Afraid he would torment her all night again, she gave in.

'He shall have her!' she said.

Back at the barber's he was able to tell him,

'Tomorrow you can send your people to make the marriage proposal and discuss the contract.' When it was day, the barber sent his messengers to ask for his young cousin and once again the godmother refused to agree.

'She won't hear a word!' they said, coming back to the barber. Then the foreigner went and tormented her again as he had done before, and this time, exhausted and terrified, she did at last agree.

'Go away, and tomorrow if God wills, it shall be done!' Next morning she told the barber's messengers that she consented. There was a splendid wedding, and that is how the barber married his cousin.

On the day the foreigner went away, he gave his friend the barber an odd piece of advice:

'Be careful,' he said, 'and don't give a night's hospitality to any passer-by.' And he said goodbye.

Some time later a man happened to go past the barber's house. He saw the beautiful young wife and his mind filled with evil thoughts. He asked the husband for a night's hospitality.

'It is not our custom,' he said, 'to put up passers-by overnight.'

'But I only want an evening meal in your stable, I shall spend the night in the mosque.'

'Oh well then, you are welcome.' He brought him in to the porch, talked with him while supper was prepared, and then the evening meal was served to them. But the guest gave a push to the lamp, which fell over and went out. The barber got up and went to fetch a flame to relight it. While he was away the guest scattered a sleeping powder over the part of the dish the barber was eating from. The lamp was relit, they sat down, but at his first mouthfuls the barber fell senseless. The visitor jumped up, forced the girl onto his horse and fled. That is how the barber's wife was carried off. When the barber woke, he looked for her in vain, the guest had stolen her.

The barber was quite helpless until one day the foreigner came to see him.

'Where is your wife?' he asked.

'Gone, stolen by the guest I took in!'

'Didn't I tell you never to welcome anyone at night?' And he wondered how he could help the barber get his wife back. Then he went into the town, bought the bits and pieces a pedlar sells and two skull caps. He put one on, gave the other to the barber, and there they were, two travelling salesmen. They went up and down and here and there calling out,

'Oh Ayyour! Oh Itri!', and these are nicknames, Sun and Moon, which husbands and wives give each other. The two friends reached the town where the wife was being held captive.

They went from door to door, calling out,

'Oh Moon! Oh Sun!' and the young wife knew their voices.

They asked the master of the house for a lodging.

'Never,' he said, 'does God's guest enter my house to spend the night there!'

'But you have nothing to fear from poor traders like ourselves.' He let them in to the passageway and stable, and they slept there till dawn. At that early hour the man got up and went to the mosque to pray. The make-believe traders called the wife and they all fled without delay.

The man came home, found the house empty, mounted his horse and set off in pursuit. Looking back, the girl saw him and cried out,

'He's following us!'

'Keep going,' said the foreigner, 'don't wait for me, I'll catch you up.' He stopped, and taking out his razor he slashed his head, his hands and face. When the rider reached him, he was covered in blood and moaning.

'Didn't two men with a woman come past here?'

'God, it was them did this to me! Let me get up behind you, we'll catch up with them and I'll get my own back!' The man took him up on the crupper, and as they rode the foreigner cut the man's throat with one stroke of his razor and threw him down. Then he caught up his friends and together they all returned to the barber's house.

He stayed with his friend ten days or a little more, then said goodbye.

A year passed. One day he said to himself,

'By God, I must test the barber's friendship. I pretended to be the Angel of Death for him, and a travelling salesman. Would he do as much for me?'

He paid him a visit and spent the night there. In the morning as he was saying goodbye, he said,

'Friend, I am ill, and people say that to cure me I need the liver of a barber's son.' Without hesitation the barber handed over his son. He took the child and sent him to the mosque to study there.

A year later he went back.

'Friend, I am still ill, and they say that if I am to get better I must have your daughter's liver.' The barber gave him his daughter, and he took her away and placed her too in the mosque school.

Next year he went back to his good friend the barber who had just become the father of another son.

'Nothing but the liver of your last-born can cure me!' he said. The barber gave him his youngest child. The foreigner took him to the mosque, where he studied alongside his brother and sister, though none of them realised this. As for the barber, he supposed that his dear friend had eaten the children's livers in order to find health.

Time passed, a year perhaps or more, and then one fine day the foreigner loaded up some pack animals with corn, barley and butter, mounted the two boys onto horses and the girl onto a mule, got onto his own horse and led the little caravan to the barber's house. Here they stopped. The barber came out, they exchanged greetings, and then he said,

'And these children, where are they going?'

'But these are your own children, the ones you gave me, and now I'm bringing them back to you. I wanted to test your friendship and see if you were grateful for the services I did you. Now we are brothers, not friends any longer!'

Should not all people of good family behave like this?

Carefree Heart

A rich trader had a daughter when he was an old man. At the child's birth he thought,

'I am rich. When I die I shall leave inexhaustible wealth to my daughter. Therefore I shall call her *El Qalb bla ham*, Carefree Heart.

The child grew night and day, both wick and lamp, and became a wonderful girl.

The son of the sultan, having heard that there was a girl in his kingdom called Carefree Heart, took it into his head to provide her with some cares. He asked for her hand in marriage, and after seven days of happiness told her that he had to go off on his travels for forty-eight hours. He installed her with all necessary provisions in a palace in the middle of the sea where she was absolutely alone.

The days went by, and poor Carefree Heart saw no husband coming back to her. She spent the first days crying, without the courage to do anything, overwhelmed by grief and despair. Then one day it occurred to her to make a model out of clay, a clay woman, and to dress it prettily. She called it *Khalti Tanna*, Aunt Tanna, and got into the habit of talking to it as if it were a real friend.

She asked its advice about everything, and

gave the answers herself.

'What shall we do now, dear *Khalti Tanna*?'

'It's dinner time, darling. Light the fire.'

'What shall we have?'

'Pound the couscous, cook it in the pot, put in some of this and some of that.'

Or perhaps:

'Today I'd really like a good *pastilla* and some *haloua* to follow. And don't forget to dry some meat for the winter.'

And in this way the solitude weighed less heavily on Carefree Heart and she felt protected and loved.

One day she was rather unwell and realised she was pregnant.

'*Khalti Tanna, Khalti Tanna*, whatever are we going to do?'

'Don't upset yourself! There's nothing to worry about. This happens to all women. You'll soon feel quite well again, make yourself some good hot soup and rest on your bed. When you're better, you can make clothes for the baby God is sending you, so that it has lots of pretty things to wear.'

When labour pains gripped her, she turned to the clay woman again.

'Don't be frightened!' she answered herself. 'The pains will pass and you will be delighted with your beautiful baby.'

When the child was born:

'Wash him, wrap him up, put him to the breast and mind you stay lying down, don't get tired. It will all work out, the man who went away will come back.'

On the seventh day:

'Today you must celebrate the baptism and give your son a name.'

'How shall we do that, *Khalti Tanna?*'

'Kill a sheep'.

'What name should we give him, *Khalti Tanna*?'

'Call him Idriss after his father.'

Three years went by and the sultan's son said to himself,

'Now I'll go and see if my wife is still alive or if care has killed Carefree Heart.'

What was his amazement when he reached the palace to see a lively little boy running towards him.

'Where does that child come from, and that woman, who is she?' he asked his wife, pointing to *Khali Tanna*. And without waiting for an answer he drew his sabre and cut off the clay woman's head. Out from its body poured a mass of worms. They were all the cares that had passed from Carefree Heart's soul into the statue.

Then the prince took his wife and his son to his father's palace, had new festivities celebrated and lived very happily to the end of his life with Carefree Heart.

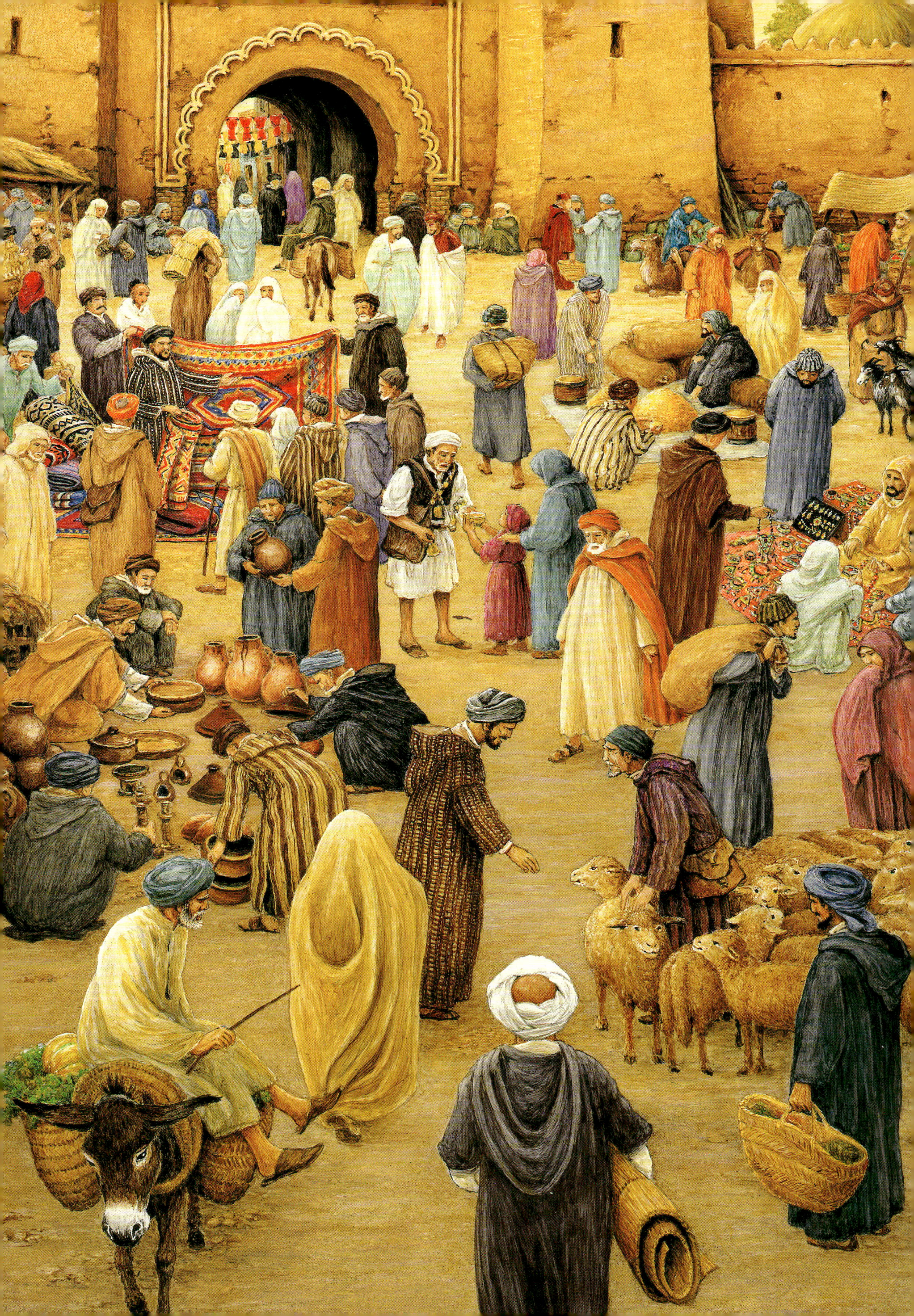

The Simpleton's Bargains

A man and his wife lived in such poverty that one day the people of the *douar* refused to let them take part in the food-sharing. The man was very annoyed at this.

'Don't get upset,' said his wife, seeing him so concerned. 'Go to market and buy some animals with the money you gave me on our wedding day.'

He reached the market at dawn, bought some sheep and began to drive them home. At noon the ewes, overcome by the heat, stood still and crossed their heads over each other to make themselves a little shade. Our man despaired of ever getting them to move again.

He was still wondering what to do when a goatherd came by with a small flock of goats. He called out,

'Hi, hey, you there! Swap your goats for my sheep?'

'Done!' said the goatherd, and the simpleton went off with his few goats. He came to a place where there were trees, and tried to gather his beasts together there, but no, off they went in every direction and started climbing up the trees to get at the leaves. He tried to get them down but he hadn't a hope, and soon he gave up and burst into tears. A man went by with an ox. He called out to him,

'Hey, you with an ox! Swap it for my goats!'

'Done!' said the man and gave him the ox. He took it and went on. As they went, a gad-fly stung the ox, and it flung up its heels and galloped into the distance. The simpleton ran after it yelling, when a man wearing a *tarboosh* happened by.

'Hey, you there in a cap, take this ox and give me your *tarboosh*!'

'Done!' And the simpleton took the *tarboosh*, put it on his head and set off again.

Soon, passing a well, he felt thirsty, and as he leant down to drink the *tarboosh* fell into the well. And when he thought what his wife would say, he burst into tears again.

There he sat, weeping, when some traders came by driving sheep and oxen and asked him what the matter was. He told them all about it.

'And now,' they said, 'if you go back to your tent your wife will pull every hair out of your beard! Hadn't you better come with us and be our shepherd?'

'Oh no! I'll go home and my wife won't say a word, she's wise and sensible.'

'Rubbish, man, all women are the same, jades the lot of them!'

'Oh no! I could have done something much stupider and she'd still forgive me.'

'Listen, we're coming with you! Once we get to your tent, you call to her and tell the whole story and we'll stay hidden. If she doesn't then say anything, we swear before God we'll give you our flocks and herds. But if she screams at you, you'll come with us and be our shepherd!'

They reached the *douar* and the men hid behind the tents while the simpleton called to his wife,

'Hallo, hey, here I am! I went to the market and I bought ewes.'

'Oh how wonderful! Now we'll be people of fashion, and we'll have all the milk we can drink!'

'Yes, if I'd kept them. But I exchanged them for some goats.'

'Oh my darling, how good of you to bring us their milk and their hair for making our tent!'

'Yes, if I'd kept them. The thing is, I exchanged them for an ox.'

'What a man you are! May God protect you for bringing us a beast which will let us plough!'

'Yes, if I'd kept it. I exchanged it for a *tarboosh*.'

'What happiness God sends us!' she said, uttering cries of joy. 'I'm afraid people will envy you. A *tarboosh*! Only palace people wear those!'

'Yes, if I'd kept it, but it fell into a well.'

'Come into the tent my dearest, God has never been so kind to us as he has today. The cap may have gone but the head is still there.'

The traders were astonished at what they heard, and they came out of their hiding place, greeted the wife and told the simpleton,

'Take our flock, you have won! Good God, we know now that there is just as much good in a woman's head as there is bad!'

The Queen and the King who was Amelknani's Son

A king had a wife whom he loved more than all the others. One day when she was dyeing her hands with henna paste she noticed that she had used too much and her hands were quite black. Afraid that the king would punish her for being stupid, she told him,

'Black is better than white.'

'What,' thought the king, who was very jealous, 'she is telling me that she loves my slave more than me!'

He killed the slave and put his body in a chest which he hid under his bed. In the evening he took hold of the chest, hoisted it up onto his wife's back, and then took a piece of rope and gave her fifty blows with it. At each one he asked,

'Who do you love most, me or the one above you?' And she, thinking of God, replied,

'You are very dear to me, my master, but He who is above me is dearer still.'

Then, supposing she meant the slave, he beat her twice as hard.

In this cruel king's city there lived a woman who had never had a child. She begged God to give her one, and God sent her an angel who said,

'You will have a son, but you must never let him eat grapes, for if he does he will die at once, as his soul is in a grape.'

The child grew up and became a scholar. One day his student friends asked his mother,

'Let your son come and amuse himself with us in a garden.'

'Never,' said his mother. 'He would eat grapes there and die, as his soul is in a grape.'

But her son kept asking till she gave in, and the young man went off with his friends. When they were in the garden they were offered a tray heaped with every kind of fruit, including appetising bunches of grapes. At first the young man refused to touch them:

'These are forbidden me, I should die if I ate them as my soul is in this fruit.' His friends laughed at him; this annoyed him; he ate a grape and died instantly. His friends wept and wept, and then they took his turban, made three knots in it, wrapped his body in it and took it to his mother. Demented with grief, she took the turban and tied it round her waist, and buried her son. Then she set off to find a person without troubles and whose heart held no hatred, who would undo the knots, which by tradition would allow her child to rest in peace.

She travelled all over the country, but could not find anyone whose heart was pure enough to undo the knots.

Then she met an old woman, who said,

'Go to the king. No one but his favourite wife can undo the knots.' So she went to the king, was taken to the queen and told her sad story.

'Only a woman who is happy and without

hatred can undo the knots in this turban, and that is why I have come to you.'

'Poor woman, you think I am happy because I am a queen! Hide behind this curtain and find out for yourself,' said the queen. In the evening the king arrived in the queen's apartments and they dined together very cheerfully. Then when all the slaves had gone the king made the queen undress, set the box on her back and asked her,

'Who do you love most? Me, or the one above you?' And as before she answered,

'You are very dear to me, my master, but He who is above me is dearer still.' And he beat her twice as hard. At last the king went away, and the queen turned to the woman who had come out of her hiding place and said,

'That is how happy I have been for a year.' Weeping, the mother said,

'When the king asks you that question tomorrow, tell him that most of all you love the king who is Amelknani's son.' Then she added, 'You can undo the knots in the turban all the same, for I know your heart contains no hatred.' And she went away.

Next evening when the king asked her the terrible question, the queen gave him that answer. At once the king stopped beating her, lifted the box off her back and went away into his own apartments to think about this reply. Then he had the slave buried at last and set off with his army to look for this mysterious king, the son of Amelknani. After a long, long journey he came in sight of a city which was completely black. The ramparts were painted black, the streets were black, the houses were black. The king halted his men outside the walls. The *muezzin*, who had climbed up the minaret to call out the prayer, saw this army and instead of calling the faithful he cried out,

'It's a countless army!'

The king there, who was Amelknani's son, asked why the prayer had not been said, and when they told him he sent for the foreign

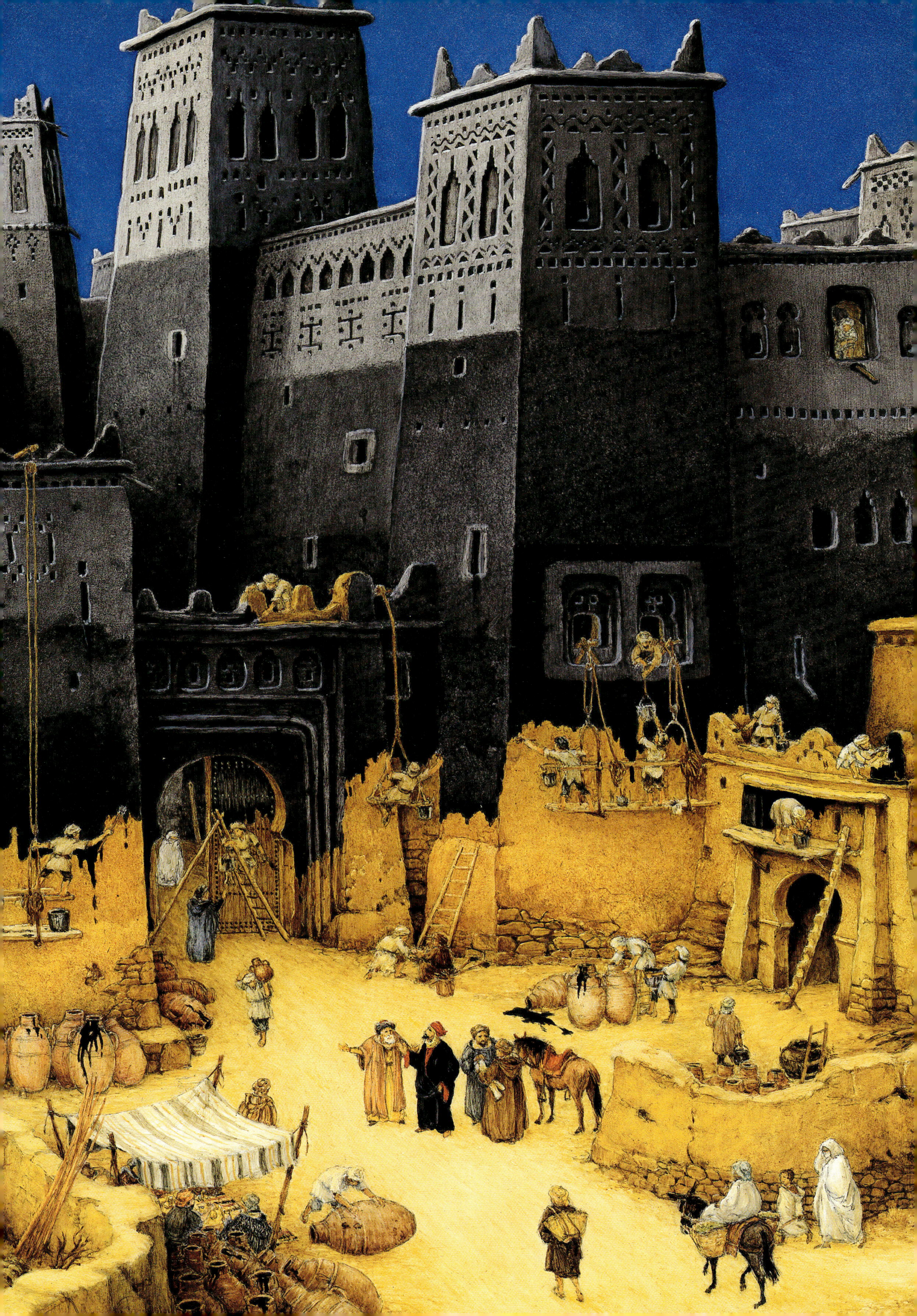

king and asked him,

'King, who are you, and why are you outside my city with an army?' Then the king told him the whole story.

'What!' said the king who was Amelknani's son, 'but your wife has done nothing wrong. Why do you torture her so? Listen to what mine did to me!

I had hardly been married a year when I realised that every evening my wife gave me a drink which put me to sleep, then she'd leave our palace and not come back till morning. One day I was telling a wise old man about my sorrow, and he said "Tonight when she gives you the glass, refuse to drink it and say, "You drink first, this time". She will drink, and then you will see what needs to be done."

Evening came and I made her drink it and she fell asleep. I wrapped myself in her clothes, covered myself in her veils, and left my palace by the terraces. Then I came to a place where a young trader was waiting, and he said, "But what is she doing, she's very late today. I do hope she has got her husband to drink the sleeping draught." I knew at once that this was the man my wife went to meet every night, and mad with jealousy I slashed off his head with one stroke of my sabre, put it in a box and went back to my palace.

Next day when my wife woke up I gave her the box. She opened it and fell dead as she recognised the head inside it. Then I had my city and my palace walls painted black and I commanded all my subjects to paint their houses black, such was my grief at the loss of my wife, whom I loved in spite of her treachery.

That is my story. Go back then to your wife and give her from me this pearl necklace, put it round her neck before you say a word, for you owe her a great deal after the way you have behaved.'

The king led his army home. The moment he arrived and without a word he fastened the pearl necklace round his wife's neck. Instantly she turned herself into a turtle dove, soared up into the sky, flew across many countries, reached the king who was the son of Amelknani and settled onto his knee. Stroking her, his fingers found the pearl necklace. He took it off and the dove, becoming human again, seemed to him lovelier than the day. He married her at once. As for the wicked and unjust husband, it sent him mad.

He Wanted to Marry a Girl who was Well Brought Up

A man wanted to marry a girl who had been well brought up. Not finding this treasure in his own neighbourhood, he saddled his horse and went to look elsewhere. He came to the gate of a town where people were playing pelota. He saw a very old man whose friends had carried him there in a basket so that he could enjoy watching the game. The rider dismounted, greeted the old man and settled down beside him. The old man sitting in his basket often cried out

'Ah, Dad's got the ball!' Surprised that this old man's father was amongst the players, the man asked him

'Uncle, your father is playing?'

'That's him!' he said, pointing to one of the players who did not look very old.

'But how do you come to be so old, when your father is still full of energy?'

'It's all my wife's fault! I hadn't been married a year when I was already an old man, couldn't even stand up!'

'And your father?'

'Ah, he married a well brought up woman. And the man who marries my sister will be lucky, for my father has trained her as he trained my mother.'

When the pelota game was finished, the man went and asked the old man's father if he could stay with them.

'You are very welcome,' he said, and took him home and showed him into his bedroom.

It was then Ramadan, and late that night the woman prepared a meal, as it is customary during Ramadan not to eat until after dark. She brought in the meal, put it down near the two men and tapped gently on the water jug to wake them. Getting up, the husband deliberately upset the dish of food. Without saying a word, the woman went to prepare another meal and came back to wake the men when it was ready. Again as he got up the husband upset the dish. He played this trick six times. Just as he was going to do it a seventh time, his guest caught hold of his arm and said,

'Accursed Satan! you really are tormenting the woman!'

'If it weren't for your sake, I would go on upsetting her meal till morning and you would never hear her complain,' retorted the husband.

The guest thought this husband was extremely cruel, and to save their daughter from being treated like this in future he decided to marry her and asked her father for her hand.

'My daughter! But she is ugly, one-eyed and peevish, you'd loathe her.'

'Whatever she's like, I'll take her if you'll agree to give her to me.'

The father agreed to the marriage, gave his daughter a sumptuous trousseau and a slave-girl, set her on a mule, and the young husband, on horseback, led his veiled wife towards his own country.

At about noon when the heat was at its fiercest, they left the road to find a little shade, and decided to wait for the cool of the evening. He helped his wife dismount under a tree and himself sheltered under another one, while the slave rested on her own. Soon the husband woke up and thought, 'Suppose I looked under her veil while she's asleep and saw whether her father was telling the truth?'

He stole softly towards her, lifted the veil and saw round her neck a magnificent pearl necklace. Her face, glorious as the sun, was as lovely as the pearls. Carefully he took off the necklace to admire it at leisure and went towards his tent, but a bird had seen it sparkle and it swooped down and took it. The man ran after it, but he was watching the bird and did not see the well into which he fell.

When the girl woke up, she saw that her husband had vanished, and called the servant.

'Where's your master?' she asked her.

'I don't know. Let's look for him.'

They searched and called in vain. At a complete loss, the young bride mounted her husband's horse, told the slave to get on the mule, and they set off again, without knowing where. Chance led them to a town, where they stopped. The girl sold the horse, the mule and the slave, bought men's clothing and enrolled at the mosque to study there.

Some time later the king heard that there was a young student at the mosque who had remarkably fine handwriting. He sent for him. The student kissed his head.

'Sit down,' said the king. He gave ink and paper to the student, who wrote a letter so well that the king was astonished.

'You are not going back to the mosque!' he said. 'You will be my secretary, you will marry my daughter and live in the palace.'

The king had the wedding performed, and when night came the false student had to tell the king's daughter the truth.

'I'm a woman like yourself. I didn't dare tell your father or he'd have put me in prison. If you wish,' she added, 'we can stay together and wait patiently until God is pleased to give me back my husband.'

'If you can wait a year, I can wait ten!' said the girl, who was much amused by the whole story.

But let's return to the husband. People came to draw water from the well he had fallen into; he caught hold of their rope; they pulled, and were very surprised to see him rising up.

'What are you, a demon or a son of Adam?' they cried.

'I am a believer who can say the creed!'

Set free like this, he wandered about until chance brought him to the town where his wife was living. He went to the market in the hope of finding work, and was engaged by a man who wanted help removing a bird's nest from his terrace. And there in that nest he found the pearl necklace. At night, as he had no money to buy food, he removed one pearl from the necklace and took it to a moneylender.

'Lend me half a *rial* on this pearl; I'll bring the money back tomorrow and you'll give me the pearl.'

The moneylender took the pearl and gave him the money, but when the man came back to pay him next day the moneylender refused to return the pearl.

'Do people of your sort have pearls?'

Very angry, he summoned the moneylender before the king's tribunal. The official in charge of the matter was none other than the young wife, who immediately recognised her husband. She invited him to spend the night at the palace, and on the pretext of drawing up the judgment, she questioned him. When he told her what had happened to him, she exclaimed,

'I am your wife!'

In the morning they sent for the moneylender, and when they threatened to cut off his head he hastily gave back the pearl. The young wife had to tell the king the truth. He was so moved by it that he gave half his kingdom to the husband and for seven times three days everyone feasted and rejoiced.

Fantastic Tales

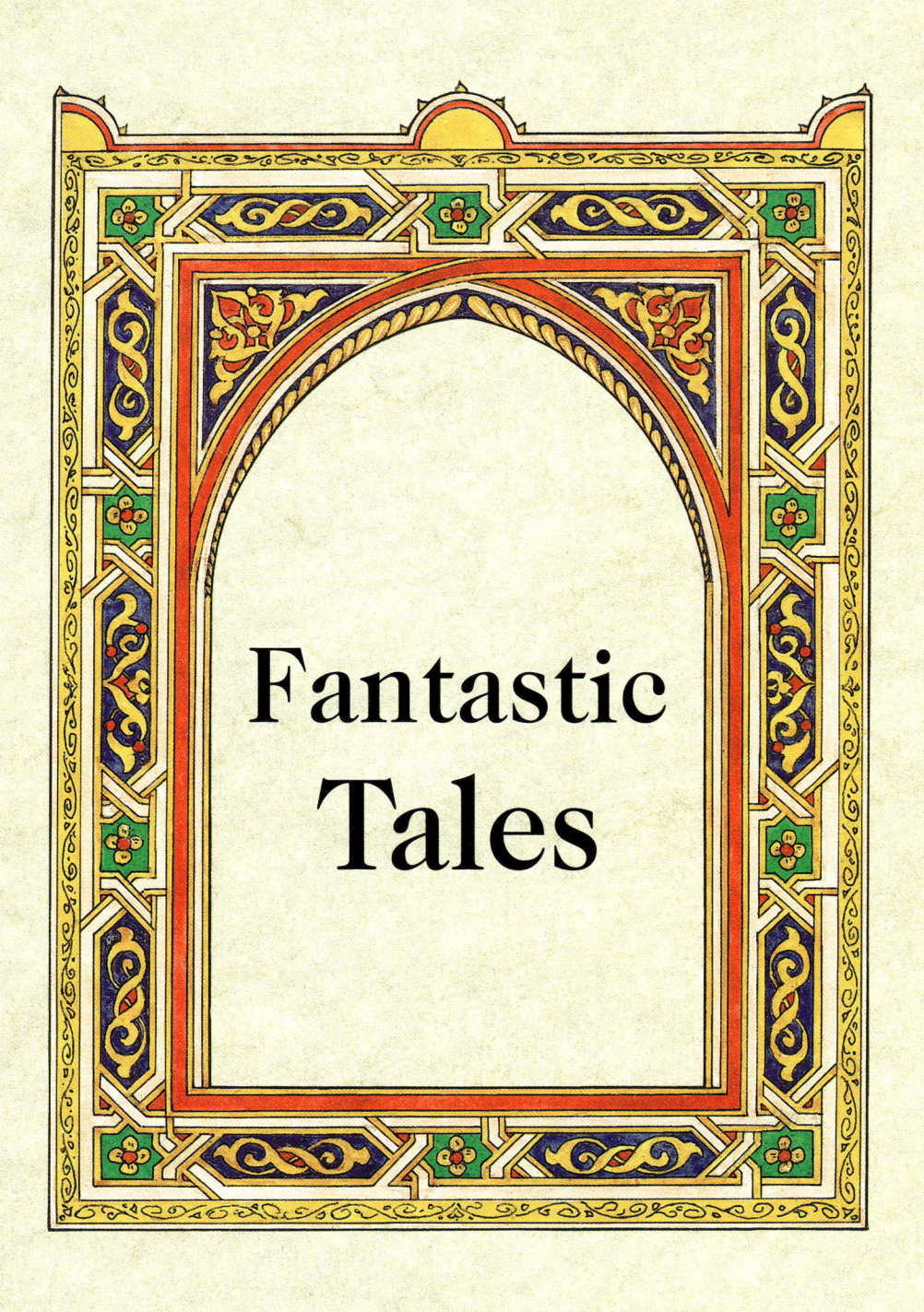

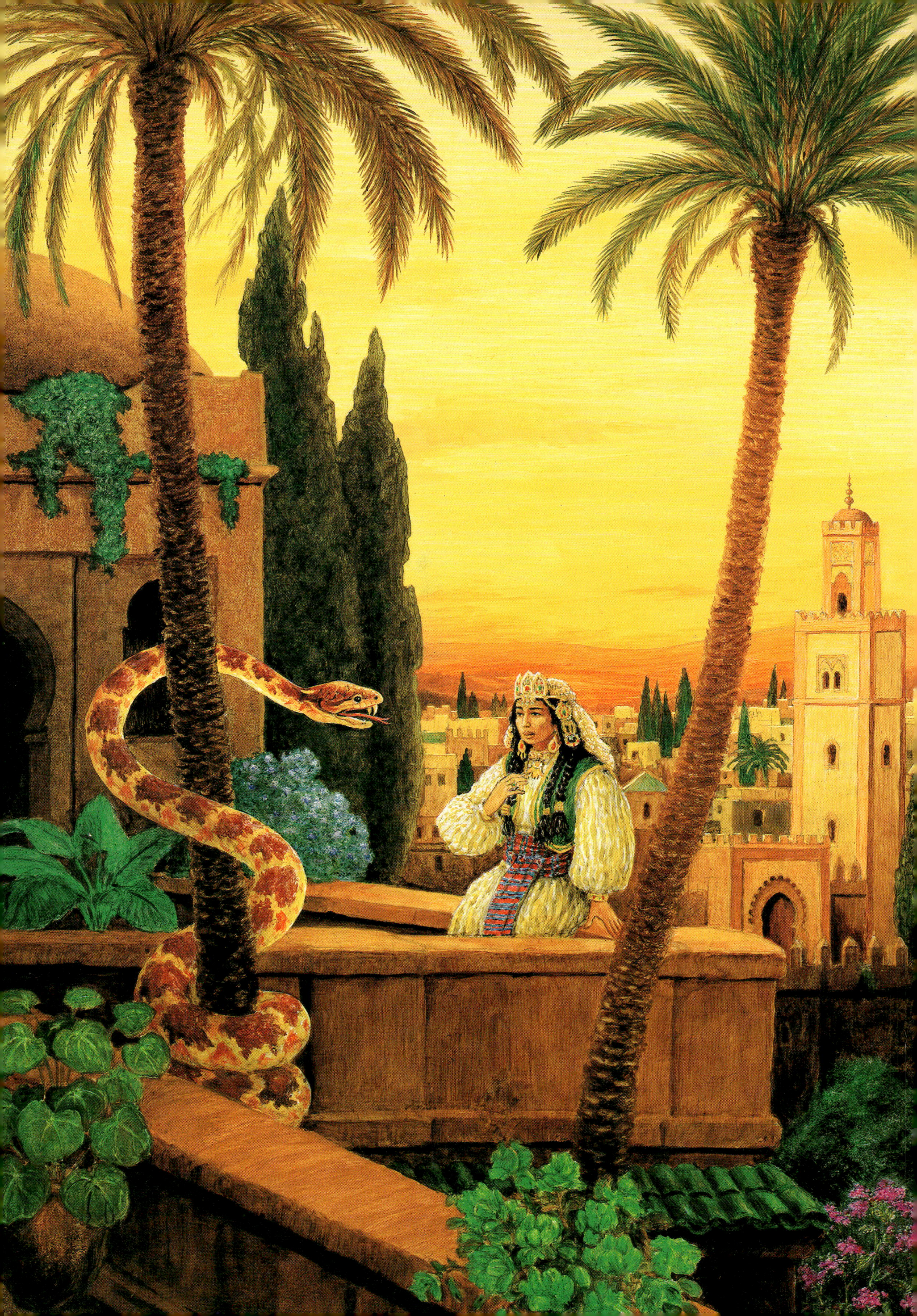

The Story of Moulay Mohammed El-Hanach,

My Lord the Snake

There was once a king married to a very beautiful queen, but they were not completely happy, for they had no children. One day the king sent for the queen and told her,

'As you can't give me a child, get ready to go away, as I am going to take another wife.'

The poor queen fell into dreadful despair. On Friday at the time of the great prayer she went up onto her terrace and at the moment when the *muezzin* called the faithful to prayer, she cried out,

'Oh my God, give me a child!' And as at the moment she caught sight of a large snake slithering in the sunshine, she added, 'Even if I were to bear a snake, oh God I beg you to grant my prayer.' And with those imprudent words, she went back into her apartments.

Some days later the queen discovered that she was pregnant and she ran to tell her husband, who was wild with delight and ordered all kinds of celebrations.

An experienced and devout midwife was found to stay with the queen until her labour began. But when it did, the queen brought a snake into the world. The midwife in horror exclaimed,

'Oh queen, you have not borne a son of Adam!' and she fainted.

The horrified queen watched the snake crawl towards her and coil itself at the end of her bed. The king was informed of this supernatural birth, but instead of tearing out his hair in despair, he exclaimed,

'Let us thank God for the son he has given us in the shape of a snake!'

During the sixth night after the birth one of the old slave women caring for the young mother dreamed about the snake, and heard it say,

'Tomorrow is the seventh day of my life, the naming day. The seventh-day sacrifice must be offered and I must be named Moulay Mohammed el-Hanach.'

Next day she told the queen about her dream, and she immediately told the king, who had it proclaimed throughout the city and the whole kingdom that he would celebrate his son's naming with a great festival and that all must come and do him homage.

The festivities were richer and more splendid than any ever seen but no one was allowed to see the child. That very evening Moulay Mohammed el-Hanach vanished, and in spite of everything the queen wept for her son the Snake.

Years passed, and one day as the queen was resting in her bedchamber a fine young man appeared in front of her and said,

'I am your son Moulay Mohammed el-Hanach, son of the king of the *djinns*. I must marry your vizier's daughter.'

Informed of this, the king sent for his vizier and said,

'No one but his mother and I myself have seen my wonderful son, and on his behalf I ask you for your eldest daughter.' The vizier bowed and said,

'Not only the eldest, my lord, but all my seven daughters are at your disposal. Choose the most beautiful.'

As soon as the wedding was announced,

great festivities were prepared and rich and precious gifts flowed in from every side.

On the evening of the wedding day the bride was led in great pomp to the apartments of Moulay Mohammed el-Hanach, where all her women friends embraced her and withdrew. The door was kept by male slaves and by the king's lovely women slaves. The husband's arrival was waited for in vain.

Suddenly just after midnight the ground cracked open in front of the girl, and a great snake appeared, writhed its way to her feet and then, shaking its coils, sloughed off its skin. In its place stood the handsomest young man, while through the same crack appeared a crowd of servants bringing in an exquisite meal in golden dishes, incense-burners full of amber and sweet scents and all the good and beautiful things which rejoice the heart. The girl instantly fell in love with her husband's beauty, and together they enjoyed the delicate pastries, the buttery *tajines*, almond-stuffed chickens and fruit from every country, each one more delicious than the rest. But at the moment of the first dawn prayer Moulay Mohammed el-Hanach turned back into a snake and he and all his servants vanished by the way they had come.

In the morning the queen visited the girl's apartments and learned of the wonderful night she had spent but also of her grief to see her husband in the morning putting on his snake's skin and vanishing. Her youngest sister who was there exclaimed,

'You must burn the snake's skin as soon as he takes it off, and then he won't leave you again.'

Next night the same things happened, but as soon as Moulay Mohammed el-Hanach was asleep his wife quietly gathered up the scaly skin and threw it into the fire, where it burned away. In the morning when the young man wanted to return to his animal shape, he could not find his glittering outer casing. He gave a shout of alarm and disappeared through a gap in the wall. The young woman waited in vain for him next night and all the nights after that. One evening she could bear it no longer and she fled from the palace. Happening to see a beggar, she gave him her rich robes in exchange for his rags, and in this disguise she walked on and on until without realising it she reached the land of the *Ghouls*. She saw a little low house and knocked at the door to ask for alms in the name of Allah. A huge and terrifying ogress opened the door. The girl understood what she was, but knew that by asking her for milk she had placed herself

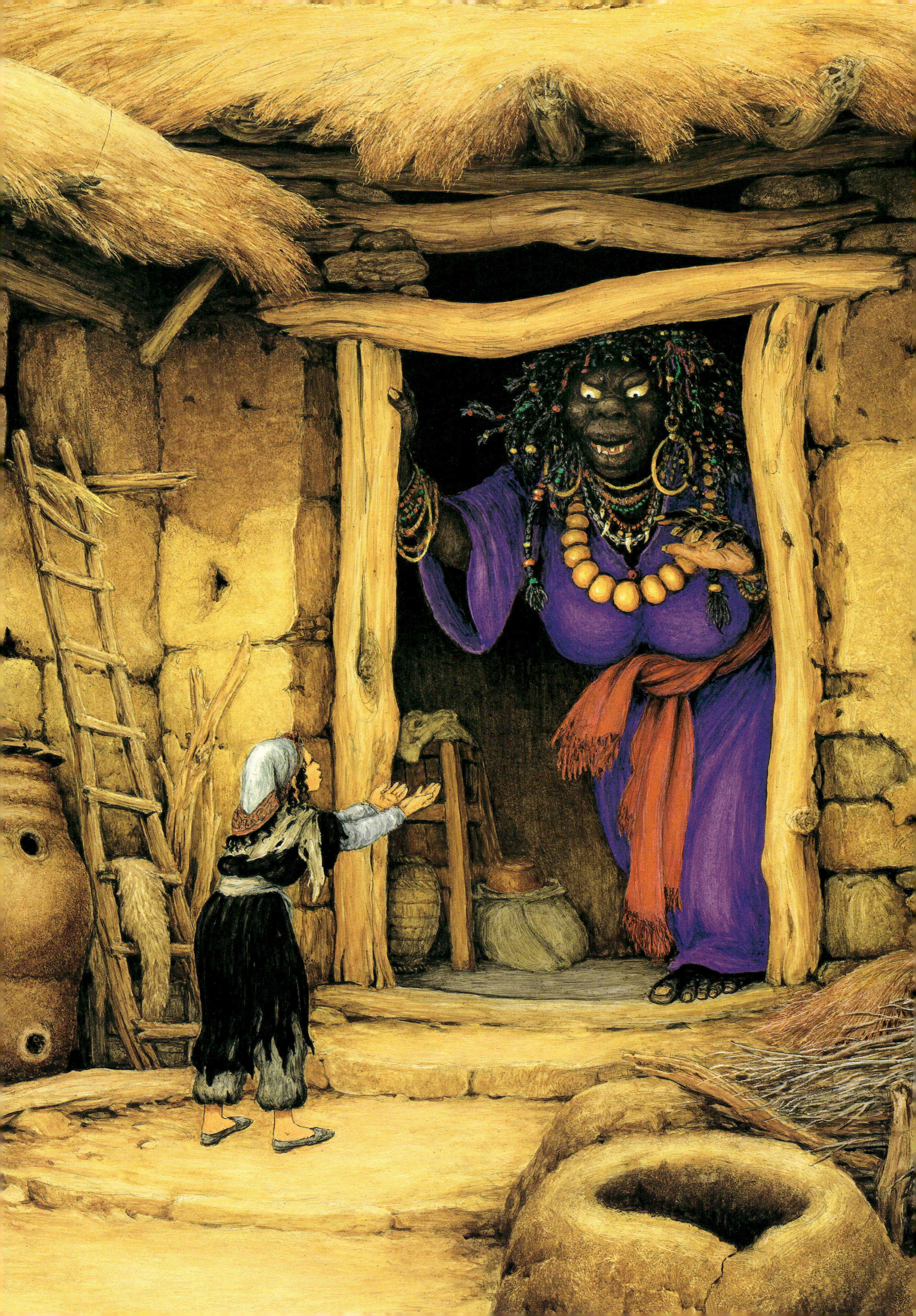

under her protection. Then the ogress said,

'You are here in the name of Allah, my child, and you have drunk my milk. I will protect you then, come and eat, and hide yourself.' She gave her meat brochettes to eat and then hid her in a large chest.

In the evening the ogress' husband came home. He was king of the *Ghouls*. The moment he entered the kitchen he exclaimed,

'I smell human flesh here, I shall have a feast', and he began to search. But his wife stopped him and told him the truth, explaining how the girl had arrived and had put herself under her protection by drinking the milk.

The king of the *Ghouls* listened, took the young woman out of her hiding place and in a voice more terrible than thunder said,

'I will protect you, guest of God, I will not use your bones for toothpicks or feast on your flesh. But you must tell me why you are here.'

The girl at once told him her story, and the king of the *Ghouls* listened to it with all his ears – which were enormous. When she had finished he said,

'While I'm asleep, you must collect the saliva which trickles from my mouth. Then you must set off and walk for seven days and reach the land of the king of the *djinns*. You will see his vizier, tell him your story, and then do what he tells you to do.'

The girl obeyed. On the seventh day she arrived outside the house where the vizier of the king of the *djinns* lived and introduced herself in these words:

'I am the guest of God and I ask for food and a bed.' The grand vizier had his door opened at once and answered,

'Be welcome, guest of God. Who are you, child, and why are you here?' And she told the whole story to the vizier of the king of the *djinns*, who listened with all his ears – which were large – and at the end said to her,

'While I sleep you must collect the saliva which trickles from my mouth and you must go into the open country. You will walk for a long, long time until you see a tall pillar. For seven days and seven nights you will anoint this pillar with my saliva and with that of the king of the *Ghouls*, and you will see what will happen to you.'

The young bride did then collect the vizier's saliva and set off. She walked for a long, long time and at last reached the pillar. She anointed it night and day for six days. On the sixth evening as she wept because she was dropping with sleep, she suddenly saw beside her a *hartaniya*, a black woman, who said in honeyed tones,

'My child, why are you crying?' The young woman, trusting her, told her all about it. Then the *hartaniya* said,

'Child, sleep in peace! I will see to the pillar while you sleep and tomorrow evening I will wake you.'

And so it was done. But at nightfall she took care not to wake the sleeping girl. She rubbed saliva onto the pillar one last time and all of a sudden the earth quaked, the pillar broke and a wonderful young man stepped out of it. It was Moulay Mohammed el-Hanach, son of the king of the *djinns*.

'You have set me free!' he cried. 'Who are you?' And the *hartaniya*, who was also a *djinn*, took on the form of a beautiful young girl and replied,

'Oh my lord, I am your humble wife and for seven days I have been doing honour to this pillar. How happy I am to have found you, and I will follow you wherever you wish to take me.' Then they set off together, leaving the beggar girl lying near the broken pillar.

When she woke, she saw how hopeless her situation was, and in despair of ever finding her husband again, she set painfully off on her return journey. All day and all evening she walked, and at last, completely worn out, reached a magnificent palace where she asked for alms in the name of Allah. The gates had already been barred, but they opened them for her and took her into a room where slaves were telling each other stories as they cleaned wheat for their young master's wedding. They gave her food, and as she was thanking the women for their kindness and getting ready to set off again, one of the girls said to her,

'It's dark tonight, and I can hear the wind in the land of the *djinns*. Don't go away, take your turn and tell us a story.'

The young woman knew no other story than her own, saddest of all, and began to tell it.

Just at that moment Moulay Mohammed el-Hanach came to see whether the wheat for his wedding had been cleaned, for this was his palace. He stopped on the threshold and listened to the whole tale without letting himself be seen. Then, very anxious, he silently withdrew, found his faithful servant and said to her,

'There's a beggar-girl in the slaves' quarters; send her to the baths, give her fine clothing and bring her to my apartments.'

When the poor wretch left the baths, perfumed and adorned, she had regained all her beauty. She saw before her Moulay Mohammed el-Hanach just as she had seen him on her wedding evening, and she fainted away. Certain that this time he had not been tricked as he had been before by the crafty *hartaniya*, he restored her to her senses with sweet scents and calling her the tenderest names. When she recovered, he heaped caresses upon her and asked her how he could be revenged on the treacherous *hartaniya*. The young woman answered,

'Use her legs to make the steps of a ladder, her arms for the handrails, and give her head to the children to play ball with.'

Moulay Mohammed el-Hanach did exactly as his wife wanted, then he promised her that he would never leave her again and would always obey her every wish. And he is keeping this promise to this very day.

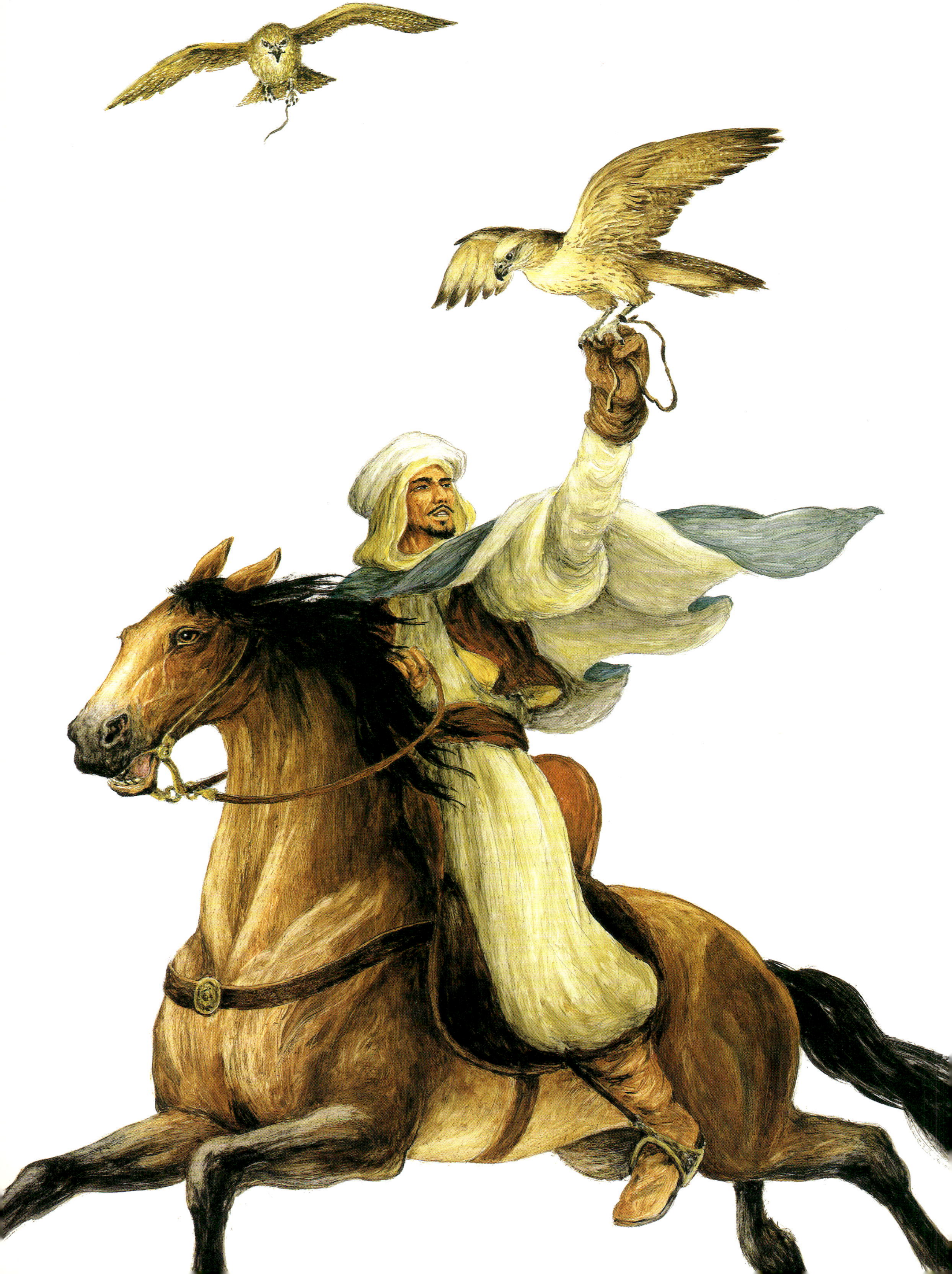

The Two Brothers

A man had two wives who gave birth the same day to boys exactly alike. One wife died, the other looked after the two children, who were so similar that she could not tell her own son and the motherless boy apart. When the boys grew to be men, they bought horses, hawks and hounds and spent whole days hunting. Their mother treated the two just the same; the meals she prepared for them to take out were always identical. So it went on until one day an old woman asked her,

'Can you tell your son and the other woman's son apart?'

'No, I count them both as my children. May God preserve them for me!'

'Stupid! You must take more care of your own son than of the other, for it is by him that you'll benefit in future.'

'But how can I tell which is which?'

'Pretend to be ill, go to bed and put some henna within reach. Your own son will hurry to you the moment he dismounts, the other will take time to fasten his horse first. When you know which one is yours, mark him quietly with a dab of henna.'

That evening the mother pretended to be ill. The young men came home from hunting. Her own son leapt from his horse and ran to his mother:

'What's the matter, mother?' he asked anxiously.

'Son, I have been ill since tea time.' She dipped her finger in the henna and marked him. The other woman's son arrived, dismounted and fastened his horse, then went in to his mother and said,

'Mother, are you ill?'

'No,' she said, 'no, I'm just resting.'

Next day as usual she prepared their lunches, putting wheaten bread and eggs into her son's bag but only barley bread into the other. Off they went hunting, and at dinner time they stopped near a fig tree by a spring. They got out their provisions. Looking at them, the son exclaimed,

'Brother, why has our mother given you black bread but I've got white?'

'It's because she's your mother, mine is dead.'

'Brother, let's go and kill her!'

'I'm not going to kill your mother, I don't want you to be an orphan like me!'

'Then what are we going to do?'

'I shall go away and leave you in peace. This spring and this fig tree will be our marker: if the tree is green and the spring full of water, you'll know I'm still alive. But if the tree is withered and the spring dried up, you'll know I'm dead.'

They parted and each went their own way.

As he rode on the motherless man passed a shepherd.

'Horseman,' said the shepherd, 'if you'll rid my flock of the jackal, I'll give you a lamb next year!'

He passed a man tending mules and donkeys.

'Horseman,' said the man, 'if you'll rid my beasts of these filthy flies, I'll give you a lamb next year!'

The young man began to hunt and he got rid of the jackal and the filthy flies for the shepherd and donkey-man. And he went on his way, still hunting.

Chance took him to the place where the king's daughter had been set out that day to pacify the ogre who roamed about near the well and prevented everyone drawing water. She was tied fast there, and at her feet was a dish of couscous and a whole roast sheep.

'Where are you going?' asked the girl.

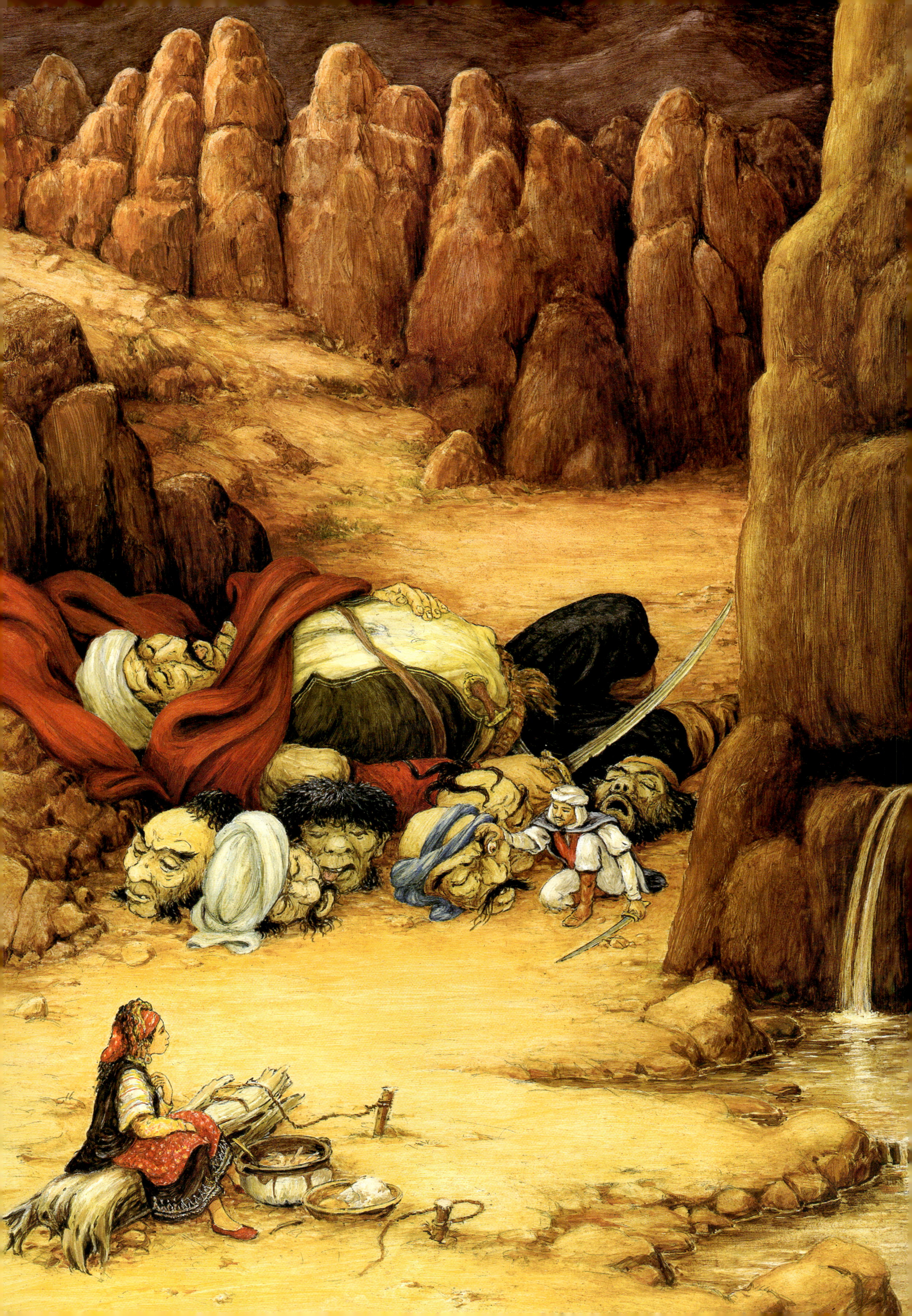

'Why do you ask?'

'Because there's an ogre who wanders about here, he'll come any moment and he'll eat you up!'

Not in the least alarmed by this, the young man calmly got off his horse and as he was hungry, started eating. His horse began to graze and the hounds and hawks went off to find food. The hunter finished his meal, untied the girl and said,

'Check my hair for lice, will you, and wake me up if the ogre comes.'

'Yes, of course,' she said, and searched his hair for lice while he fell asleep. She was not thinking about the ogre at all, when suddenly he appeared. She could not manage to wake the hunter; then she cried, and one burning tear fell onto the young man's face and woke him. He jumped up and exclaimed,

'Didn't I tell you to wake me if that beast turned up!' He swore and threatened her, 'If I didn't fear God, I'd finish off you and the monster together!' The ogre interrupted,

'I'm the one you want, come on!'

'Oh, donkeys fighting each other!'

The ogre drew his sabre and raised his seven heads; the orphan drew his, and made seven caps stand on his head. The battle began. Whenever the ogre slashed off one of his caps, he slashed off one of the ogre's heads. Six he cut away, and at the seventh the ogre said,

'Cut it off!'

'I'd rather God cut my hand off!' For he knew that if he cut off the last head, the other six would grow again. The ogre fell dead. The hero cut him to pieces and took one of his shoulders, which he gave to the girl. He also gave her his sword, his ring and a slipper, then rode away.

Those who had been watching this exploit went to tell the king. The girl too went off to tell everyone, and shouted to the terrified people who had fled the city,

'Come back, come back, the ogre is dead!' And to reassure them, she showed them the ogre's shoulder.

The king commanded his soldiers to summon every man in the country, every single one. When they were all assembled, he told them,

'I intend to give my daughter and half my kingdom to the man who defeated the ogre. Here are his sword, his ring and his slipper. The man who can draw the sword with his little finger and whom the ring and the slipper fit, that will be my son-in-law!'

People scrambled to try the tests. They were offered the sword; not one could draw it with his little finger. They were offered the slipper; it would fit none of them.

'Look,' said the king, 'is there anyone else who hasn't tried?'

'Lord, only one man, but he is a long way from here, on the mountain.'

The man was brought. And he drew the sabre with his little finger, he put on the ring and it fitted him, he put on the slipper and so did that.

'Get to work, women, feast the betrothal!' said the king. 'I give him my daughter and half my kingdom!' And he commanded a great celebration for the wedding.

One day the king warned his son-in-law,

'Take care you don't get lost in the forest, there's an ogress in there who eats all who go near her.' Some time later the son-in-law thought, 'After all, why shouldn't I go hunting in that forest?'

And in he went. He killed a hare, and was just getting ready to roast it when the ogress appeared.

'Son,' she said, 'let me have some fire!'

'Come nearer.'

'I'm afraid of your horse, your hawks and your hounds.'

'Come on, don't be afraid!'

'If they were tied up, I wouldn't be afraid. Here, take this hair and hobble them.'

When they were hobbled, she ate them all up one after another.

Let's go back to the other brother. A year had passed since the two brothers parted. One day when he went to the hunting rendezvous, he found the fig tree withered and the spring dried up. 'Something has happened to my brother,' he thought. And he set off at once to look for him. On the way he met a shepherd,

'Come and get your lamb,' said the shepherd, 'the one I promised you last year.' Now the young man knew that his brother had passed that way, and he set off again.

A man tending donkeys and horses called out to him,

'Come and get your lamb, the one I promised you last year.'

He went on with his journey, asking for information as he met people, and in due course came to the king's city. The king went to meet him and said,

'I'm glad to see you, my son! When you didn't come back, I was afraid you had gone into that forest!'

'I don't know what you mean. Where is the forest?'

'Over there, a long way off!' Then the young man thought, 'That must be where my brother died.'

'Go and cheer up your wife,' went on the king, 'she is so anxious about you.'

He went into his brother's house. His wife, taking him for her husband, flung her arms around him, and she brought him his supper which he ate without comment. At bedtime he washed and then prayed at great length.

'Good God,' said the wife to herself, 'what's the matter? Is he never coming to bed?' He prayed and prayed, and she at last fell asleep. He kept on praying, then stretched out on the matting until the shepherd's star appeared in the sky. Then he got up and went into the forest.

He ransacked every corner of it and at last found the remains of a fireplace,

'There,' he thought, 'that's where my brother built a fire.'

He killed a hare and prepared to roast it. Busy lighting the fire, he did not notice the ogress arrive.

'Give me some fire!' she said to him.

'Come nearer,' he said.

'I'm afraid of your horse, your hawks and your hounds.'

'No need, don't be afraid!'

'If they were tied up, I wouldn't be. Here, take this hair and hobble them.' She gave him a hair from her head.

He went to his horse, and while he was pretending to hobble him he said,

'Smash her head, make rags of it!' He went to his hounds:

'Go for her feet!' To his hawks:

'Pick out her eyes!' But he warned them all that he would make mincemeat of any one of them that attacked her belly.

'Come along!' he said at last. She did so; the animals all attacked at once just as their master had said. The ogress collapsed. He sliced open her belly and took out his brother, the hounds and the hawks, senseless but not dead. The young man considered what could be done for them. He sat down and saw two little lizards fighting just in front of him; he watched them. One of them knocked out the other, then went away and found some leaves which it brought back and made the other breathe, and at once the tiny creature was restored to life. The young man then gathered this plant, and when he had as much as he needed he made his brother breathe in its smell, and the horse, the hounds and the hawks too, and they all woke out of their sleep. The brothers recognised each other, embraced, and went back together to the king and told him the whole story.

'You are welcome, my dear sons,' he said. 'I am getting old, one of you can take my place and other can be his vizier.'

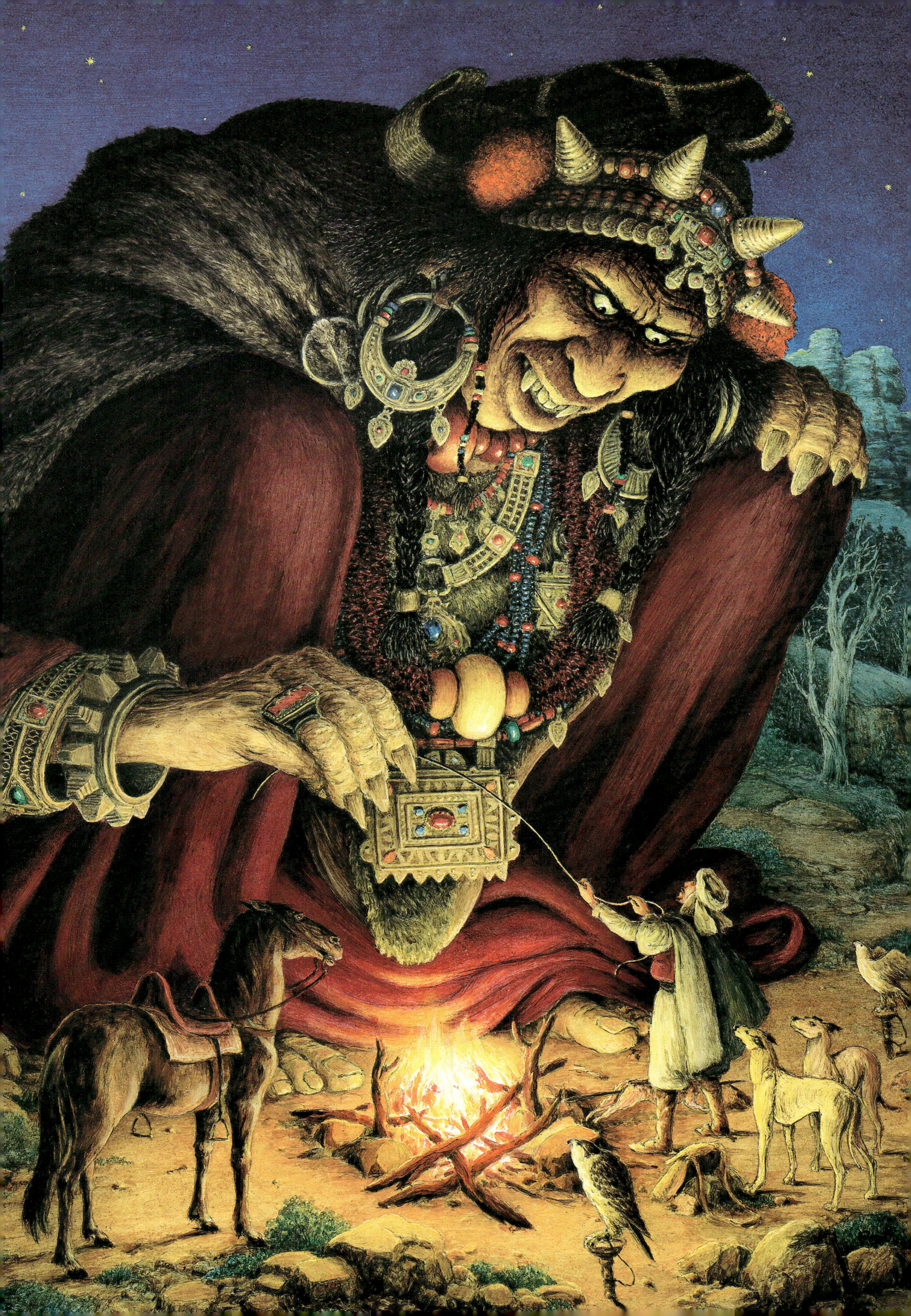

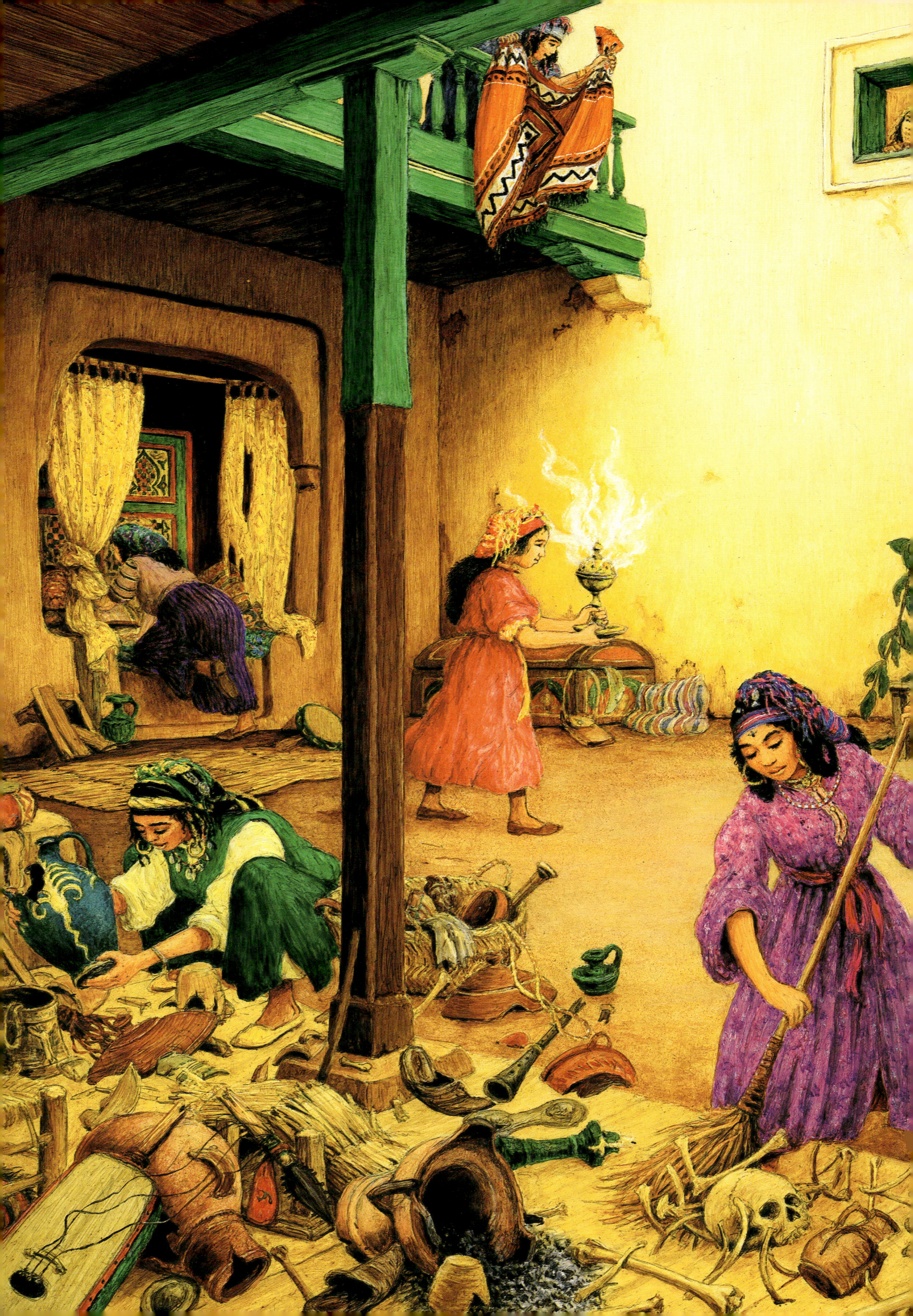

The House Where You Die

There was a man who had two wives and each of them gave him seven daughters. Fourteen daughters and not one son! This is exceptional bad luck! Their father liked one of his two wives much better than the other, and the one he liked best was a wicked woman whose only wish was to get rid of her rival's children.

Now in this town there was a house frequented by *djinns*; anyone who spent a night there, died. The wicked wife heard about this deadly house, and she persuaded her husband to rent it and to send the seven daughters of the despised wife to sleep there. And this was done.

But they were good brave girls, well brought up and what's more very shrewd. They were quite untroubled and simply asked their unhappy father to buy them brooms, some fish, milk and perfumes.

The house was dirty and full of the dried-up bodies of men who had perished there. Bravely the seven sisters swept everywhere, flung milk on the floors to pacify the *djinns* who loved this drink, as they knew, and burned perfumes for the same reason.

Meanwhile one of them had lit a fire and was grilling fish for their supper.

But then lo and behold, a hand without an arm, without a body, appeared and reached out towards her, while a soft pleading voice said,

'Sister, oh sister, give me some fish to eat!'

'Certainly, my dear, I'll be glad to,' said she cheerfully. 'This one is still too hot, it would hurt you. I'll cool it down for you' After a

69

moment she put the now lukewarm fish into the hand. And she did the same for seven other hands which appeared one after another.

Evening came, and the seven sisters lit candles and sat down to table. A *djinn* with two noses then appeared, with a candle in its hand. Instead of being frightened, the seven gave him a friendly welcome, made him sit down with them, and offered him mint tea with plenty of sugar.

'Can a creature with three noses join you?' cried another *djinn*, appearing suddenly.

'Yes, of course, come in.'

And one after another in came *djinns* with four, five, six, seven noses, to all of whom the sisters gave a kind welcome.

Then a little child's voice was heard weeping and wailing,

'Oh my sisters, my sisters, please, bring me down!'

The bravest of all the sisters took a candle and went up the stairs leading to the terrace. There on the last step lay a big piece of meat. That was what was making all the noise. She took it gently in her dress and carried it downstairs.

Instead of harming them, the *djinns*, touched by the welcome the seven sisters had given them, thanked them for having fed and perfumed them, for cleaning the house and keeping them company.

Next day at dawn the father arrived at the deadly house together with fourteen porters bringing seven stretchers to carry away the bodies of what he thought would be his dead daughters. But instead of lifeless corpses, he found them well and cheerful and covered with the jewels given them by the grateful *djinns*. He had to send away the porters and take the girls home.

And who was sorry? The wicked jealous wife. Seeing all the gifts the *djinns* had heaped on her step-daughters, she wanted the same for her own girls and told her husband he was an idiot. She insisted that he take his seven other daughters to the deadly house and leave them there alone, and so he did.

Like the others, they asked for fish and food, but as they were lazy and dirty they did not think about brooms or perfume. Without doing any cleaning, they began to prepare their meal. Suddenly a hand was stretched out to the girl who was grilling the fish and a gentle pleading voice said,

'Sister, oh sister, give me some fish to eat!'

'How horrible!' cried the girl, and she began to recite the exorcism, 'In the Name of God, kind and merciful! I seek with God a refuge against Satan the stoned one!' And to her sisters she shouted, 'Bring me an axe!'

But at this threat the hand vanished.

When the *djinns* with two, three, four, five, six and seven noses appeared to ask if they could share their meal, the sisters instead of giving them a kind welcome rejected their company, not forgetting to heap them with insults and mockery. When the child's voice begged from the terrace,

'Help me, bring me down!' no one went near the piece of bewitched meat but they all cried out,

'God damn you!'

And when the father arrived next morning at dawn, this time without porters or stretchers, all he found in the deadly house were seven corpses.

Bitterly did he repent of his error and ceased to love the wicked wife whose evil purpose towards her step-daughters had caused his grief.

The Girl and the Ogress

There was once a young orphan girl. As she no longer had anyone in the world to help her, she went into the forest to gather wood. She got a big bundle together, set it on her back and began to go home. But as she did not know the forest well, she could not find the way, and began to cry. Suddenly there in front of her was a beautiful woman who said,

'Why are you crying like that?'

'Alas, good mother, I am an orphan, I have come into the forest to get wood and I can't find my way home.'

'It's all right, child, cheer up. Come with me and you can be my daughter.'

And the two set off and walked a long long way through the forest.

But night came, and the girl saw that the woman taking her away had turned into a huge ogress, with breasts hanging down to her knees and teeth as long as a baker's oven peel. She was terrified as they went into the ogress' lair, and said to her,

'Oh mother ogress, don't eat me. I'm thin and wouldn't make you a good meal. Let me be your daughter. I will prepare your meals, and when you go into the forest and bring back good meat, I will cook it for you.'

'All right,' said the ogress, 'I won't eat you till you get fat.'

So the days passed, the ogress searching the forest for food and her 'daughter' keeping house and doing the cooking.

One evening the ogress came in. She had gone to and fro in the forest all day long but had found nothing there for dinner. Then she called the girl to her and began to poke and prod at her.

'Oh, oh,' she said, ' you're nice and plump. This ear is just ready for roasting, it's time you were cooked!'

'If you would be so kind, mother ogress,' the girl answered, 'as to wait until I've washed before you eat me! My hands are dirty and I want to go and bathe. You get your invitations out, and cook me tomorrow.'

So the ogress went to invite her friends and the girl seized her chance and ran.

She walked all night and came to a large house which looked lived in. Going inside, she went all round it without meeting a soul. Then she went up a long staircase and into a bedroom full of wool, where she hid, thinking, 'If ogres live here, they will come tonight, and I shall be done for.'

Night fell, and a pack of ogres arrived all

72

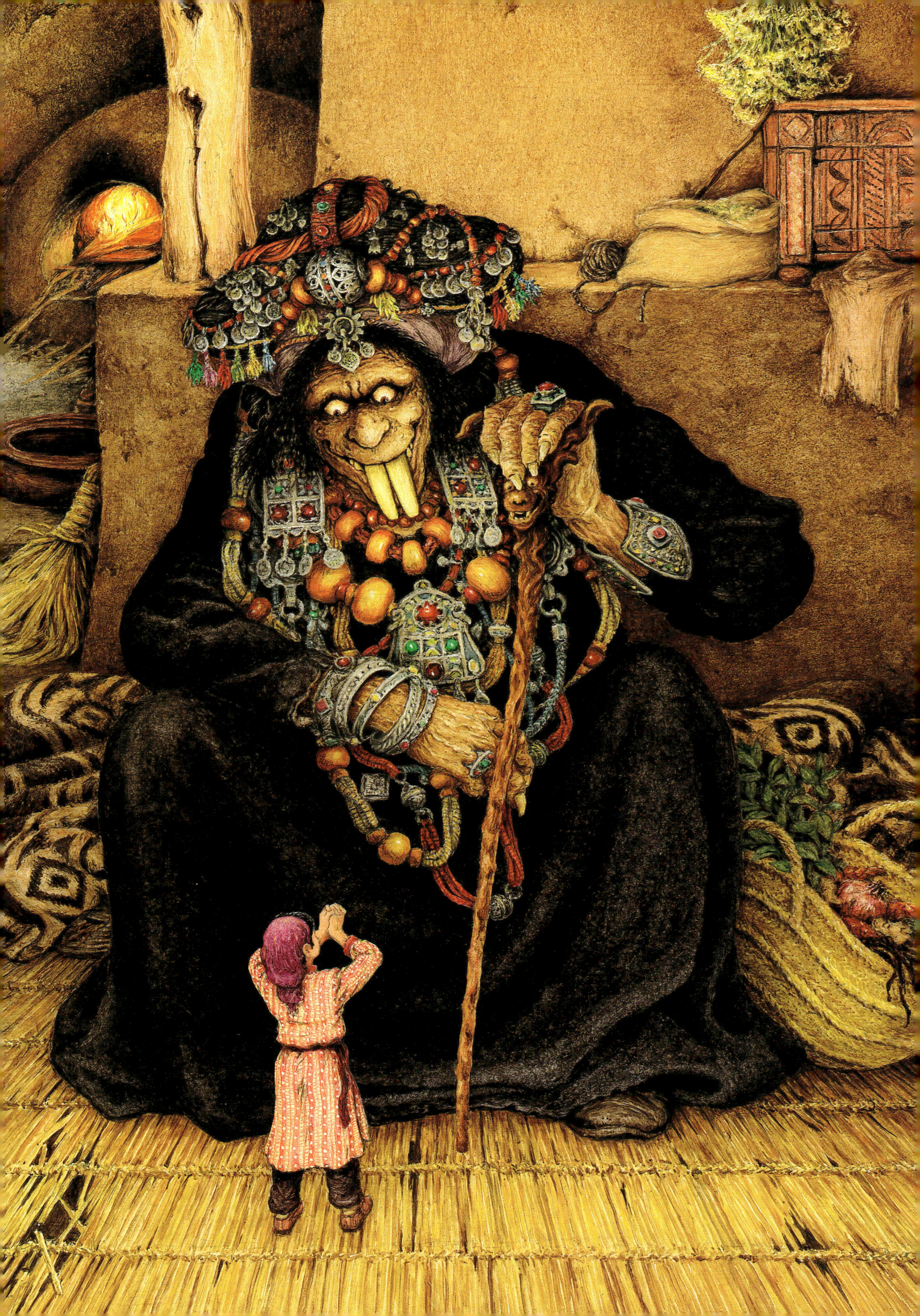

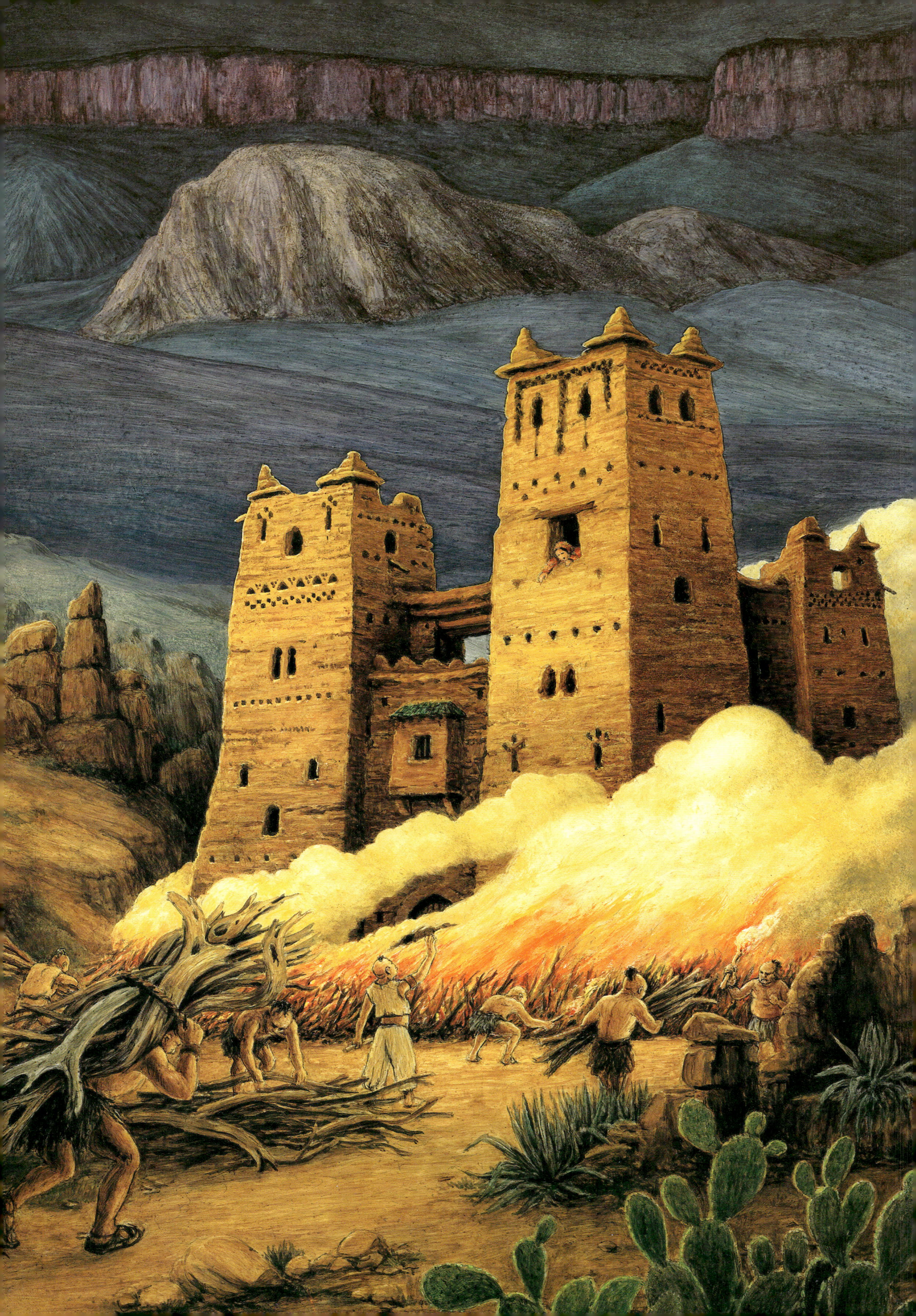

singing for joy, so well had they fed. They could certainly smell human flesh but they looked all over the house without finding anything. As they had eaten heartily, they fell fast asleep.

Next morning they woke, took on the appearance of human beings and set off into the forest.

Then the girl went downstairs, shut all the doors, fastened all the bolts, and went up onto the terrace. Evening came, and when the ogres returned they couldn't get in, and they heard the girl laughing aloud on the terrace.

'What are you laughing at and where have you come from?'

'I have come from God who put me down here, and I am laughing because it's up to you to make a good meal – I am plump and ready for roasting, and I ran away from my mother the ogress who wanted to eat me up. But my fate is written! Go and get wood, build a fire by the wall here, and when the embers are glowing red, I shall fall into it and all you will have to do is roast and eat me.'

The ogres went off at once to get wood, built the bonfire and set it alight.

The flames leapt up everywhere, licking the walls of the tower where the girl was standing. One of the ogres called to her,

'What are you waiting for, daughter of Adam, why don't you fall into the embers?'

'I am waiting till you shake the wall, all of you ramming your heads against it as hard as you can. Then the wall and I will fall down together.'

Stooping down all together, the ogres tried to ram the wall with their heads, but the wall was so hot that they suffered terrible burns and all died then and there.

The girl watched from the terrace. When she was sure they were all dead and the danger was over, she came down and began to search through the house.

In every room she found huge wealth. They were crammed with boxes full of jewels, with clothing good enough for kings and queens. Sacks of gold were heaped up in the hallways. In the cellars she found enormous jars of oil and of butter. In the stables there were great flocks and herds, the storage pits were brimming over with barley and wheat. Dazzled by all these treasures, the girl knew that she would never be poor again and that there was more than anyone could need to live a happy life.

A little later she heard a loud hammering at the door.

'Who's there?' she asked. It was a young and attractive trader in spices lost in the forest at nightfall and trembling as he looked for shelter. He was afraid he had come upon an ogre's house and was delighted to have found this lovely girl, who told him her story.

The two young people fell in love, married, and lived happily together until it was time for death, who parts lovers, to come to them.

Glossary

Bâb Mahrouq: *the north-west gate of the city of Fez, over which the heads of executed rebels used to be hung.*
Cadi: *a judge.*
Djinn: *a spirit of the air, good or bad, born out of fire.*
Douar: *a collection of nomad tents, an encampment.*
Ghoul: *a blood-sucking ogre.*
Guembri: *a two or three-stringed musical instrument made of wood and covered in sheepskin.*
Haloua: *an eastern sweetmeat, halva.*
Hammam: *a bath-house.*
Hartaniya: *a black woman from the oases in south Morocco.*
Moucharabieh: *a wooden or metal open-work screen put across windows.*
Muezzin: *the man who proclaims the time of prayer from the top of a minaret.*
Pastilla: *a Moroccan dish consisting of flaky pastry filled with almonds and pigeon meat, served hot.*
Riad: *a walled garden inside a building.*
Rial: *former north African currency.*
Tajine: *a popular Moroccan meat dish, cooked in a pan with a pointed cover.*
Tarboosh: *a red cap with tassels, worn by men.*

Acknowledgements

The stories collected here by Philippe Fix are adapted from the following traditional material:

From *Popular Tales and Legends of Morocco* collected in Marrakech by Dr Légey:
The Story of Old Âref ou Aqel, *The Story of Bartal and Jerâda*, *The Woman and the Cadi*, *The Man with a Stupid Wife*, *A House Bought in Paradise*, *The Queen and the King who was Amelknani's Son*, and *The Girl and the Ogress*.

From *New Tales from Fez* published by Mohammed el Fasi and E. Derrmenghem:
Weeping and Wailing, *The Language of the Birds*, *Princess Saktsa or Maskoutsa*, *Carefree Heart*, and *The House Where You Die*.

From *Berber Tales of Morocco* by E. Laoust:
The Stolen Treasure, *Wit is the Best Weapon*, *Fair Shares*, *The Barber in Love*, *The Simpleton's Bargains*, *He Wanted to Marry a Girl who was Well Brought Up*, and *The Story of the Two Brothers*.

*Printing completed in September 2003
by the Jean Lamour Press.*